DEATH
is a
MIRACLE

A Daughter's Contemplative Memoir
of Her Father's Transition

WINN MALLARD

BALBOA
PRESS
A DIVISION OF HAY HOUSE

www.DeathIsAMiracle.com
Cover image "interpenetrating panels" and all other illustrations (except where noted) by Anna Trodglen Copyright 2015 Wildpic Art Publishing. www.annatrodglen.com
Author photo by Bridget Ferguson www.bridgetferguson.com

Balboa Press books may be ordered through booksellers or by contacting:

Balboa Press
A Division of Hay House
1663 Liberty Drive
Bloomington, IN 47403
www.balboapress.com
1 (877) 407-4847

Print information available on the last page.

ISBN: 978-1-5043-4709-9 (sc)
ISBN: 978-1-5043-4710-5 (e)

Balboa Press rev. date: 4/4/2016

DEDICATION

This book is dedicated to death...
the grim reaper... resurrection...
our greatest teacher...
the whole point...

And, of course, to sweet daddy-o.

A Prayer...

Oh sweet goodness… beloved wonder of wonders…
godgoddess…
Hold us tenderly as we journey
through the miraculous and the mundane…
Guide us to always be present to the Now…
So we might rest in the riddle
And accept the struggle…
While feeling the shivers of anticipation
As the illusion of separation shatters
Bit by bit.

With eternal gratitude for all that you give us in every now moment,
Amen!

CONTENTS

PREFACE

As I sit in my Asheville log cabin, cozied up against arctic temperatures, working to birth this book before returning to Peru... I must say that I am utterly amazed by the path that brought me to this present moment, amazed and immensely grateful. Had my path not curved and twisted in its various (often mind-boggling heart-breaking) branches, I would not have landed on my parents' stoop at precisely the opportune moment... landing equipped with a well-supplied belt of spiritual tools and the flexibility to change my life and be present. To be present for a spiritual initiation like none other.

I had not yet given much thought to my parents dying. Oh, occasionally - when someone I knew lost a parent - I would imagine it, but never for more than a moment. I had spoken to my parents about death, keeping it mostly abstract. I would relate mystical experiences I'd had via the shamanic tradition I worked with in Peru. A spiritual tradition referred to as "a death practice." They were sort of interested, mom much more so than dad. But I hadn't envisioned one or both of them actually doing it, dying that is. It's fascinating to me how I carried on hardly noticing this large looming inevitable crack in the support of my reality just hanging around nonchalantly... sitting there ready to split and bust open the dam, rip through the fabric, just plain turn the world upside down!... and once it did, altering my spirit in a way that currently feels unfathomable to comprehend.

Everyone loses their parents. It is a given, a rite of passage for us all. Therefore it is an opportunity for everyone to grow spiritually and personally. And the way we hold it, as individuals and as a culture, determines whether or not it becomes a spiritual initiation. My deep heart desire is that everyone in the world might have the chance to experience such an initiation, and if putting my words out via this little book might inch us in that direction, then I rejoice.

My entire life, since I was a small child, I have had an intense and passionate desire to help humanity move to a kinder and more harmonious relationship with the natural world. This passion led me to explore eco-spiritual teachings which guided me to the world of the divine feminine. From there, beloved Sophia - Lady Wisdom - brought me back to Christ as the embodiment of Unity.

Now, I claim my mission as one to help awaken Christ consciousness within myself and humanity. Christ consciousness is Unity consciousness, an awareness beyond duality or separation, which is the heart ushering in the harmony I've been dreaming of since childhood.

In Unity consciousness death becomes transition. In Christ consciousness death is resurrection. I pray that we might all recognize and embrace the gem of wisdom that crystallizes through our witnessing… through our sitting… through our midwifing… the miracle of death.

ACKNOWLEDGEMENTS

Always first, I open my heart in gratitude to my sweet goodness, my most cherished beloved, my godgoddess, for the love force that nourishes my life in every way. I love you to the ends of the all, my glorious wonder. I am yours!

Secondly I wish to acknowledge my sweet mama, Gatra. She was most certainly the one "holding it down" during daddy-o's long death march of 233 days. Her perseverance and loyalty, patience and kindness were exemplary, both to him and to me. While I was writing creative updates, Gatra was writing the amount of urine and time of flushing – the catheter, that is. While I was reading books about death and dying she was warming up daddy-o's soup and spooning it into his mouth. At least two meals a day for 233 days equals a heap o' spoonin'! She never wavered. You're amazing mom. Your gigantic heart and immense fortitude teach and inspire me... always! Thank you for everything!! I love you!

Next I want to thank my brother Reid, the gentle knight in shining casual wear. His clarity and thoughtfulness held the scene in a firm yet flexible embrace. And his phenomenal patience and willingness to do whatever was needed guided the rest of us as we aspired to follow in his stead. Thank you Reid, most especially for holding me the moments I needed to release. It was remarkable being part of the daddy-o team with you! I love you!

And to my brother, Rob, whose reverence, devotion and honoring of daddy-o, and his process, set a very high standard while shoring up the walls with integrity so that the family embrace, the container holding daddy-o up, was strong and durable, thus giving him the support he needed to march his march. Your earnest respect and acceptance, Rob, along with your drive to do the right thing, the kind thing, shines brightly for me... a star to set in my life compass. I love you!

And to my scrumpdillyicious Uncle Cole, daddy-o's brother, who at intervals, plopped down into the scene like a sweet nugget of divine delight bringing humor and lightness into the fold – an imperative ingredient. Dear Cole, your adoration of your brother and your sweet heart-felt desire to keep him as long as possible, celebrating the life he had left, was crucial to the story. I cherish your insights. Thank you! I love you!

And to my sisters-in-love, Alison and Karen, who were never too far away, thank you both for the personal support. I am so grateful for the deepening of connection. I treasure and love you both dearly.

On May 31st, about 3 weeks after daddy-o took to his death bed, Coleman Terrell Lewis transitioned. The Lewis family moved in next door to the Mallards when Coleman was a toddler. Our two families have shared greatly over the years and this year, 2014, the sharing went to a profoundly deep level as we lost our youngest and our oldest. In sharing such grief our thread of connection has become even more intimate. Thank you Luther, Martha, Claire, Beth and Coleman! My life story, the Mallards' story, is far richer having shared a driveway of heart and soul with you all! I love you all deeply.

I want to express great gratitude to all the beautiful people from the ripples rippling out that kept us in their prayers and sent love through food, flowers and messages during daddy-o's death march. There were so many; most especially from Glenn United Methodist Church and the Emory/Druid Hills communities. Thank y'all so much. A well connected community of loving exchange fills like nothing else can.

Norkeyta was the hospice aide who came every day Monday through Friday taking care of daddy-o, cleaning him up and making sure everything was okay. She always was enthusiastic and cheerful and handled daddy-o with incredible compassion. We couldn't have done it without you, Norkeyta! Thank you!

Carol was the hospice nurse who helped mom and me as much as daddy-o, really. She guided us in invaluable ways and daddy-o always felt better to know she was on her way to check in on him. Thank you, Carol.

I am so grateful for all my beloved friends who looked out for me in miraculous ways. You know who you are – my lucky charms fell right when I found each and every one of you!!

I want to send appreciation to Roberto (aka Wow) and all my Peruvian clan, keeping Casa de Wow!!! afloat and holding space for my return after so many moons away. Gracias Wow... you have taught me so much through los buenos y los malos... the root and what it means to be connected so deeply to place... a los apus y pachamama... and how to love loosely with true acceptance... giving it up to the mystery moment by moment... te amo.

I have had so many amazing spiritual teachers in my life, all of whom contributed to my spiritual tool belt in remarkable ways. Right now though, I want to acknowledge two whose presence I felt most deeply during this initiation. Carol Parrish-Harra, my Esoteric Christianity teacher, was living through a similar journey with the death of her beloved husband. Her teachings felt like a bit of buoyancy keeping me from sinking. Thank you Carol. And to EzMaRa, my guide and energy mentor in Peru; without the insights and teachings and clearings, along with our skype dates, I probably would not have been able to go the duration and open my heart as fully to be truly present to the remarkable journey. Thank you EzMaRa.

The other spiritual teacher whose teachings were with me every step of the way is the plant spirit being, ayahuasca. Through my shamanic work with her in Peru she offered me a peek into the death journey, an experience that proved invaluable while sitting with daddy-o during his. Thank you gracious one. I am eternally indebted to you for the insight and expansion you have shared with me. You are a high priestess!... (and thus, not to be taken lightly).

Great thanks to Anna Trodglen for her wonderful illustrations!!! In her words – "I am an artist who attended the Glenn United Methodist Youth Group for a couple of years in the 1980s where Dr. Mallard often led us in song. We sullen teenagers were transfixed and heartened by his enthusiasm for singing and we all enjoyed singing together with him. It was a bright spot in the week gifted to us by a presence of light in our lives. My mother, Roberta Bondi, taught with Professor Mallard at Candler School of Theology for over twenty years and they enjoyed a wonderful friendship. I am deeply honored to be part of his special daughter Winn's book." Right back at ya, Anna – the honor is all ours!

And last but certainly not least.... Daddy-o!!!!!!!! Oh my goodness, my beloved father, teacher, advisor, friend... I don't know what I did to get so lucky pulling your name out of the hat but I'll take it! And I will work the rest of my life to exalt your presence in me and sing gratitude unto the hills with glory everlasting! Thank you for gifting me your bounty of spiritual riches, throughout my life. And most especially now, thank you for gifting me the magic and wisdom and vulnerability and truth and beauty and love of this, your final walk. I can't imagine a more exquisite account of human meeting divine. And that I had a front row seat makes my heart explode with humility and wonder and gratitude. Thank you sooooo much! You are my hero, my example extraordinaire. I love you!!

INTRODUCTION

This book is a collection of facebook posts. They begin Monday May 5, 2014. I had been staying with my parents, Bill and Gatra Mallard, since the previous March 15th returning to my tap root for an extended visit from my new home in Peru. Daddy-o had been declining but mama would talk of it on the phone like it was something they were gonna fix. She would say to me, while I was sitting in my wee adobe room in the heart of the sacred valley of the Inkas, "Don't worry, we'll have him fixed by the time you get here." Then I would talk to him and his words would lead me to wonder about her words. Not as much what his words were, but how they were, so flat and dull and unenthusiastic.

Six months or so prior, in August 2013, Bill and Gatra had moved out of their home of 50 years. The stairs were becoming too difficult for both of them to maneuver and the house just too big and needy for them to keep up. The idea was that the youngest son, Edward Robertson (Rob), would move in with his family which allowed my parents an easier and more gradual shift. It was a win-win situation all around. And even though the best scenario, it was still a hard shift for daddy-o.

Structure kept him afloat…. a creature of habit…

Routine and roots… familiar reserve…
well-oiled gears of 50 years…

Pumping to fill the well…

Gone.

Several months following that tremendous change mom and dad went out to visit Lawson and Margot Crowe in Boulder, Colorado. Lawson and daddy-o became best friends when they were 14 and had remained so throughout the years.

They were two of a three musketeer's team including Gordon Binns. Gordon had crossed over years prior. Dad had been present at his death and then a few days later rolled right into the role of officiate at his funeral. Well, the same thing happened with Lawson. That was November.

Boom! another great change… beloved soul friend…

The trinity -a hard hobble with two, impossible with one…

72 years of laughter, singing and leaning…

Gone.

More than a minister, or certainly as much so, daddy-o was a teacher. It was his passion… his fuel… his wind… his Ruah (breath of god). Since he had retired from teaching at the university he had continued filling his sails teaching Sunday school, the Live and Learn class. It was a fitting end to his teaching journey in many ways. And still another major letting go! He just couldn't get around so good… hard to stand and talk… hard to sit down and get back up… wobbly… shuffling insecure footing… "Maybe we need to take a break while tests are run. Perhaps the doctors can fix him." That was December.

Sigh… the shuffle has won… his teaching is done…

Gentle wave as Bill Mallard the teacher takes leave…

No pomp No ceremony…

Just sails lay flat…

The breath that filled them - Ruah…

Gone.

Daddy-o had decided one of the ways to keep strong and fit was to walk two miles in less than 30 minutes every morning. And to this discipline he kept a vigilant commitment for as long as any of us can remember. It was his morning groove laying the track for daily routine. It gave leverage to the day ahead. A firm nod to the need for order and structure. And then one morning he fell. While walking his fast walk, his daily groove, he fell… splat! Splayed out on the ground unable to pick himself back up, helplessly waiting for someone to see him and call for help… Ouch!! This was in January.

Bamm! Knock down!! swift and furious alteration…

2 miles in less than 30 minutes…

Arms swinging… legs pumping…

Signature stride…

Gone.

All of this change in a mere 6 month time lapse is mountainous for a man of 86 years. Not long after the fall, which resulted in no physical injury, Gatra reported him saying, "I feel that the life force is draining out of me." Shortly after I arrived he said to me, "I feel the role of Bill Mallard is over but I've had so much fun I don't want to go."

William Mallard Jr. (Bill) was born on May 28, 1927 in New York City to a sweet southern flower of a mother, genteel and delicate, Carrie Lou Born and to a charismatic and brilliant father, bigger than life and gruff, William Mallard. They lived in a penthouse overlooking central park west. Southern transplants from Georgia, they were carried on the winds of a northerly gust for the big city career whirlwind with skyscraper views. William Sr. was a lawyer and Carrie Lou's father had directed her to accept his proposal as he seemed to be "the steadiest of all her suitors". And in some ways it was true. Unfortunately family success was short lived. After 2 years of separation, Carrie Lou, toting along the 6 year old Bill Jr., boarded a train for Nevada as it was the state slated for uncontested divorce.

During the separation process, Daisy Dean Born, Carrie Lou's mother, having lost her husband, Early Winn Born, rode the northern current up to the big apple swooping in as a formidable and stout presence to wrap the horrified and ashamed single mother and her young boy child in a protective and grounding embrace. This embrace lasted until Bill was 14, as did the education fund from his father. During those "Daisy Dean years", Bill attended the most prestigious elementary school in Manhattan (also all boy all Jewish) Columbia Grammar, where he excelled. It is interesting to think of him as a minority child, the only Christian being brought up by teetotaling southern Methodist women. Apparently he was never allowed to go to any of his friends' bar-mitzvahs for his maternal guardians had caught wind that wine was consumed by the parents as part of the celebration. He also never saw his father.

When he was 14, Bill's rock and angel of strength and fortitude, died. Every year he talks about Daisy Dean on her birthday, telling us how old she would be, with a glossy aura of distant adoration. It's incalculable to imagine what his insides felt as he said goodbye to her and to his familiar NYC. His mother thought it best to move after Daisy Dean's transition choosing Richmond, Virginia as they had some distant cousin in the area. My sense is that the shame of the divorce always kept them from moving back down to their Georgia family. And, as it turned out, Richmond proved to be a fine place for Bill's adolescence as a great mother hen was sitting on her nest waiting for him. That hen was Reveille United Methodist Church. The youth group offered him his two cherished comrades, Lawson and Gordon, and the church mothers and fathers scooped him up as one of their own giving him strong capable guardians once again. They financially supported him through college, Randolph Macon, as well as through his post-graduate work at Duke Divinity, writing the expenses into the church budget.

After getting his PhD in theology, Bill got a teaching job at Sweet Briar College for a few years before landing at Candler School of Theology, Emory University, Atlanta, Georgia in 1957. And here he stayed until his retirement in 2000. He married one of his students, Gatra Mathews Reid of Andalusia, Alabama in 1961. They spawned three children: Reid, myself and Rob, raising us in the aforementioned home a 10min walk from campus.

Daddy-o always walked to work.

So as a newborn, he plopped down into this world, eyes opening in a strange northern land, floating in a chalice with damaged and wobbly parents, no recognizable heritage, no community and as an anomaly school boy with little connection outside of his books and studies. Yet departing from this world, he takes leave from an overflowing chalice of love and connection, a full-bodied heritage and sense of place, a deeply adored and abundant community all reflecting a life well lived. His remarkable legacy being all the individuals he knew and touched throughout his walk, as eventually those human connections, with their puzzle pieces of insecurity and confusion, delight and amusement, took over his books and studies, and became his true divine grace.

This contemplative collection of facebook posts sprang into being as an effort to inform the collection of adored and adoring humans - his legacy. After a while though, they became more than that and took on a life of their own. My greatest hope is that they honor him and continue his life's mission. A mission of sharing the love of Christ, the wisdom of Unity, and the joy of Mystery, to every being he encountered.

And I saw a new heaven and a new earth.

- Revelation 21:1 (RSV)

"A new heaven" is the emergence of a transformed state

of human consciousness,

and "a new earth" is its reflection in the physical realm.

- Eckhart Tolle

In light of this outlook and the unfolding of Luke's whole account (his Gospel plus Acts), the conceiving of Jesus by Mary through the Spirit is the very beginning of that new creation, the onset of a process that will embrace the world. Its significance is not only intimate and personal, but cosmic. God, the Most High is going back to the depths and giving a fresh start to all things everywhere. The spirit initiates the new creation in the virgin conception and then invites all to enter it by inaugurating Jesus' ministry at his baptism, descending "upon him like a dove" (Luke 3:22).

- *Bill Mallard (aka daddy-o)*

1... "OH ME"

"oh me"... is the theme of my life right now as
this is daddy-o's constant expression...
he has begun his journey to the other side and i
suppose all that seems appropriate to him is "oh me".
he is at home... comfortable and peaceful and
somewhat responsive for small moments...
someone is by his side at all moments... at this moment
it is me.

he has been such a stupendous spiritual warrior in
this lifetime... has brought so much lovelight into this
world... and now he is facing his last challenge...
it is time to take his armor off and allow.
time to go home.
he loves prayer... all that you can send him for
an easy and graceful transcendence will,
i assure you, be received.

he just spoke in his dreamy state and said –
"we must cross the bridges we come to"
and then he said "oh me"...
lovelovelove

Swing low sweet chariot
Coming for to carry me home
Swing love sweet chariot
Coming for to carry me home.

I looked over Jordan and what did I see
Coming for to carry me home
A band of angels coming after me
Coming for to carry me home.
-traditional spiritual

2... WITH WONDERMENT
WE GIVE PRAISE

speaking for sweet daddy-o
and the rest of us here holding his hand...
thank you all so much for the incredible loving
attentions and heart speaking reflections...
each and every morsel has lifted us...
we truly floated today...

dad's "oh me's" turned into gentle silent
acceptance... resting easier...
in between valued visits from beloveds and intimates...
the homeplace rang with tears and adoration...
laughter and stories...
with singalong spirituals to end the night...

we hold immense gratitude for this day... all is well...
each moment a precious part of the journey...

with wonderment we give praise.
lovelovelove

In her book, The Wisdom Jesus,
Cynthia Bourgeault speaks of the resurrection:

The real point is this: what Jesus does so profoundly demonstrate to us

in his passage from death to life

is that the walls between the realms are paper thin.

Along the entire ray of creation,

the 'mansions' are interpenetrating and mutually permeable by love.

The death of our physical form is not the

death of our individual personhood.

Our personhood remains alive and well,

'hidden with Christ in God' (to use Paul's

beautiful phrase in Colossians 3:3)

and here and now we can draw strength from it (and him)

to live our temporal lives with all the fullness of eternity.

3... HOVERING BETWEEN WORLDS

this Wednesday morning daddy-o let us know he needed
more silence... so the theme for the day became moving
our energy and presence to match his... to watch and
feel for the subtle signs of his transition and support
them and him... so that he might go where he needs
to go freely and unencumbered... no longer taking
care of us or shifting his energy to match ours...
low lighting... soft voices...very gentle touch...

it is astounding to feel the potency of being extremely
aware and present within a cocoon of deep intimate
vulnerability... the greatest honor i will ever know.

our beloved bill is making this journey with absolute courage
and humility... it is gorgeous and most certainly will end up
being his greatest accomplishment... that is since the one
that brought him into this world. he and i said today that
god's two greatest miracles must indeed be birth and death.

please continue sending him your thoughts and prayers...
he is comfortable and peaceful
and he is hovering between worlds.
lovelovelove

4... HALLELUJAH HOSPICE AND "OH MY WHAT A SURPRISE!"

well today, Friday may 9, has been a two
theme day for the daddy-o team...
hallelujah hospice... and "oh my what a surprise!"...

hospice in-home care – what a wonderful sign ringing
the chime of our budding new consciousness...
acceptance, compassion, and love professionally
packaged and delivered to our door...
gratis! freebe! we gotcha covered!

our case manager nurse came and explained... of
course everyone gets to have their own style and we
never predict... but we can anticipate some things that
are common and get an idea of a time window...
not to mention a little box of emergency meds, ohmy!

though so far daddy-o is drug free...
and really his only discomfort has been the hiccups.

So hospice sez... hiccups happen... we can think of it as the
body's pulling in one direction and the personality's pulling
in another... and there in the middle sits the diaphragm
pulled in both directions thus spazzing out... hiCCup!

and Bill already knew because last night he said to me
in response to "daddy-o are you comfortable...?" "No! My
body wants to go in one direction and the rest of me in
another... this is not a situation of comfort".... "oh me".

6

hospice nurse also said... he could be here for
longer than what we might currently see...
with ups and downs - "rallies and declines"... and indeed...

"oh my what a surprise!" he got a hankerin' for tomato
soup and cheese toast followed by chocolate ice cream...
what a comfort feast, eh?... we were blown away!...
after almost four full days of mini-sip mini-sip... 90% cool
clear water... daddy-o rallied with three of his favorite
earthly delights... and afterwards wanted a shave!!

so we receive the grand and constant reminder to always
rest in the mystery...
it is all so far beyond us...
so much bigger than our minds might ever grasp...
all we can do is sit in our hearts radiating compassion
- the acceptance of all that is.
until tomorrow...
lovelovelove

5... RIDING THEOLOGICAL RAMBLINGS THROUGH THE SHADOWS

well it is Saturday afternoon,
though really time has no meaning right now....
and I like to think that where daddy-o is soon to be
time will also be a non-issue.
Our nights have been blurring into days and visa versa...
dad really hasn't gone into a deep sleep since Monday
and night time has been when he is most active.

Daddy-o and I sat up all night riding theological ramblings
through the shadows.... He was the professor, of course,
and I wasn't just a student... most of the time I was a
whole class of students... and it was so wonderful for
me to actually see him in action one last time...
bill mallard - the fun, inspiring, creative,
incredibly entertaining, super smart
and most importantly, ohsokind teacher!!
and boyhidee did he LOVE doing it!

As of today I would say he is probably at least
¾ of the way over to the other side...
early this morning he had a few moments of panic
as he felt himself falling...
I said to him he was falling away from his body
and into the hand of god
there was nothing to be afraid of...
He responded
"well winndy, there's just no improving that statement"...

8

we talked a good bit about that and ended up
comparing it to one of his favorite plays
"Waiting for Godot"…
And so we continued referencing it…
Godot
and waiting and trusting and releasing and allowing…
And so he is…
And as he has done all things in this lifetime…
he is doing it with conscious grace…
and I must say it is the most beautiful thing I
have ever had the pleasure of witnessing…
may he be a teacher for all of us in this his final lesson…
lovelovelove

6... GENDER INCLUSIVE WORD FOR MIDWIFE?

so monday afternoon... and all is quiet.
daddy-o has mostly been sleeping since sunday morning
about 5am... it is a change for he had not really been
sleeping all week... he must have needed a break...
so we are all taking little breaks along with him.

his waking moments within the break also include wanting
to get back to life's routines... (hospice would call it a
"rally")... daddy-o loved his routines... he used them to
give him the structure and strength he needed to walk his
amazing path... yesterday afternoon he wanted to do his
leg exercises and get up for a while. we accommodated
his desire and very quickly he was ready to get back in
bed... he asked what day it was and we said "sunday
mother's day" and he said "of course!"... and started us
into a chorus of 'happy mother's day to you'... afterwards
exhausted he slept until this morning and upon waking
he wanted to come out into the living room and have his
breakfast... we told him that just wasn't possible right now...
a little while later he told the hospice nurse he
was frustrated for he felt he had no initiative
or choice in things...

so feeling deeply the struggle and trial of it all...
letting go of choice... letting go of the routines...
just letting go of it all...
and my heart is busting with amazement witnessing
the strength and courage he is mustering to be able
to let go with awareness and consciousness...

10

perhaps it is harder this way but what a gift it can be
when we walk through our challenging moments
sober and clear and completely present...
feeling and knowing each fear and hurdle...
with a confidence that facing them
without looking away or numbing ourselves...
will indeed bring an unconquerable inner peace...

reid my brother and i had a beautiful discussion
yesterday regarding our roles as midwives...
(we need a new gender inclusive word for this role –
reid is busting through the old barriers!! as usual).

there is such a fine line between allowing dad to be in his
journey - to not pull him back towards the earthly world...
and to, at the same time, not rush the process in any way.
our culture has had such a great fear around death for
so long that it is very difficult to not unconsciously resist
it even when it is looming so closely and is obviously
so natural and right...
and our concern is we do not want to make what is
already the most challenging task of dad's life
more difficult...
so this is a great part of the trial and struggle
for the daddy-o team...

we feel so incredibly grateful to have the love bubble of
community support that you all have been contributing
to... we truly are lifted by the energy and prayers we are
receiving and are confident that this journey would not
be near as graceful and smooth without this bubble...
our gratitude is eternal!
lovelovelove

What the caterpillar calls the end of the
world, the master calls a butterfly.

- Richard Bach

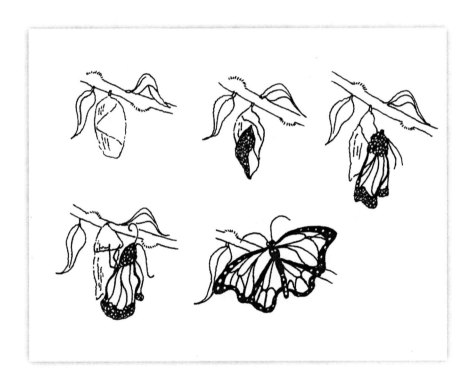

13

7... THE GENTLE POWERS

Oh my goodness… I finally left our wee little condominium
world this day, Wednesday the full moon of may… Over
the past 10 days I have only left twice for perhaps an hour
or so… Just now I walked over to lullwater preserve – one
of atlanta's secret gems… I found myself moving very
slowly with intense sensitivity… the songbirds singing
directly into my ear… the breeze sweeping my skin,
caressing each pore… the meadow of white clover
sending me into a drunken swoon of sweetness…
the green of life hugging me in a brilliance of vital love…
the gentle powers speaking to me in volume!

Daddy-o taught about the gentle powers… it is one of
his main themes… and I realize that being immersed
in sacred journey with him for so many days
awakened a deeper awareness in me…
a new level of receptiveness to the sacred…
most especially the gentle powers…
gentle miracles each and every being…
including the breeze.

We had a rough patch with sweet daddy-o this past
Monday night to Tuesday afternoon… It was a 19 hour
spell of arduous work for all of us… his catheter was
malfunctioning and it made him extremely agitated…
almost to the point of rambunctiousness…
Hospice nurses were called and sister
morphine invited in to work her magic…
and between the two – earnest nurses and opium
in a dropper – things finally simmered down…

The ordeal took its toll on all of us… most especially
daddy-o. The case nurse looked at me and mom,
haggard as we were, and suggested we move dad
to the hospice residency unit so we might have help
with the care-taking details. Immediately we both said
"No"… holding to our hope that he remain home…
Though I must say if we let hospice take over I think
he would have a very high ride… they are not at all
afraid of the rock-a-bye narcotics… in fact, they have
even given us those raised-eyebrow-lowered-eyeball-
out-the-corner-down-at-ya-"say what!?"-look
when we have said he is medication free…
I snuck in a mini poke reproach "I just don't know
how people died before the mighty pharma chariot
was available to carry them home"… with a winkwink
nudgenudge… "swing high sweet chariot."

Tonight daddy-o was muchly renewed we are happy
to say… he even wanted a bit of nourishment…
mom and I also got good rest… And so we continue
to rest in the mystery… allowing each day to be
what it is and sending gratitude for all of it…

As I was leaving lullwater preserve it began to rain… I
walked down to the edge of the lake and watched the
drops falling in… a plop then a bubble and then the
perfectly round circle spreading out until it vanished into
the all… it made me think of us humans… we plop down
into the mighty world as wee individual drops spreading
out through our lives until we eventually just expand into
the great and mighty all… Expansion into Pure Love…
what a nice plan…
lovelovelove

From *Language and Love:*
Introducing Augustine's Religious Thought through the Confessions Story
by William Mallard (daddy-o)

He [Augustine] did become convinced that

all humankind (as he knew it)

was seeking this wisdom, the single truth of God.

Is that too lofty a view of humanity?

No, he decided, since all humankind is certainly seeking happiness.

And what is happiness but to rest in an immortal wisdom,

a deathless good,

the passionate love of truth?

Truth alone endures and provides a happiness that cannot be lost.

8... TREASURING EACH STAGE

Friday morning May 16.... And today I feel sad for really
the first time within this remarkable waxing moon phase
of may during which I have been a handrail to daddy-o's
stairway of ascension...
and I'm probably sad because daddy-o is sad...

Our journey began Sunday evening May 4
and my interpretation is that for the first six days or so
dad was in an altered state...
he was wonderfully out there!
What some would call hallucinations...
I call straddling the veils.
What others would call delusional...
I call tapped into other dimensions.

And he traversed the worlds like a pro!
He was so clear within it all and fearless...
empowered and accepting...
mostly resting in his role as professor and scholar...
using the language he used when wearing that garb–
amazingly eloquent and diverse vocabulary...
absolutely gorgeous!

A small regret is that we did not have a tape recorder....
but then I trust that those moments were not supposed to
be captured... just as his spirit needed to wander freely
with little or no constraint...

Of course we had to keep him in bed…
so all the transition moments when he needed to get
to the next seminar… off to perform a wedding…
or dismiss a class and move on…
we had to unfortunately interfere…
but he would re-bound quickly into the next program
or discussion group…

It all was an exciting and entertaining adventure…
and what would really blow my mind was how he would
connect with visitors from where he was within the ride…
totally knowing each person with clarity, wit, kindness
and sincere enthusiasm.

And, of course, he was having visits from non-earthly
beings also… perhaps angels and ancestors… he would
look up into the air somewhere and with glee say
"well looky who's here!"

My sense is that dad was also very psychic during
these times… super sensitive and aware of the feelings
and thoughts of those of us surrounding him.

I felt a more real and intimate connection with daddy-o
during these days than I reckon I have ever known…
his unguarded vulnerability and raw authenticity
gave me a vision
of what must really be god's truth for human beings…
and my gratitude is limitless.

Over the weekend he shifted out of the altered
state and progressed to what now feels like a trial
of acceptance within the normal human state…
wrapped in all its defenses and gooey attachments…
and as we might expect, with this state of
consciousness has come confusion and sadness…
and a sweet neediness.

He's become very clingy to Gatra
(who has been an incredible spiritual warrior throughout
all of it – more about her amazingness another day)
and keeps asking "how did I get here..?"

Last night he told Gatra he was looking for
a righteous god… this morning he said to her…
"I know I am supposed to be going somewhere"…
And a little while later, "Okay let's get on with it…
close the hatches and get the wheel turning."

Oh dear sweet daddy-o…
always earnest to do what you are supposed to do…
indeed embodying a precious innocence
from a bye gone era.

We are treasuring each stage…
every exhilaration and every challenge.
lovelovelove

8.5... REID'S WORDS

Hello friends. I have just shared three posts of my sister's from last week (the 3rd attached to this), in part, because I want to share her fluid, poetic ramblings of writing, but, mostly, as they nicely reflect her/our experience, perspective, feeling, and events of last week as we all continue this journey with dad. Gratefully, dad is still with us, and at this point appears he may be for a little while, a week, several weeks, one really can't predict these sorts of things, but when you have been counting the days, a couple of weeks seems like a nice long time. A friend of mine commented that dad's "ups and downs" - the good days, followed by the tough days, followed by the good days, and on and on - had to be stressful. I'm sure at some point that would become stressful - preparing yourself, then releasing, preparing yourself, then releasing... I have heard it before, and I'm sure it's true. But really, for me, at this point, the "not knowing" is not hard. I'm grateful to just have another good day with him, and we, the family team, will figure out the tough days. Dad remains generally confused or out of touch with his situation, or should we say has a different understanding about his situation. He's not always certain where he is, understands he is sick but that's about all, nevertheless, he remains completely oriented to all of us around him and any visitors that come by. In fact, he is a pleasure to be with. With little prompting he will sing with you, recite a Bible verse, or chuckle about the past. He remains Mr. Humility, so affirming of those around him, so sweet, particularly when asking for reassurance that he is doing everything he is supposed to be doing through this process, rather than pushing back against what he doesn't seem to fully understand. An understanding of all of this, if it does come to him, must come in pieces. On Saturday he called us, my mom, brother, sister and me to his bed. It appeared he so sweetly wanted to clarify his apparent realization that he now needed to be in our care. He described coming to a "comforting, pleasant awareness of being received by the three of you and mom... I very gratefully received the idea and fact that I had moved into you all's hands". He then so carefully asked each of us for reassurance that he was reading this right. We all affirmed his new understanding of this, he paused, looked up and uttered, "That is impressive and beautiful." ... Oh, my sweet dad... In the midst all of this, what a poignant moment of my life with him... A beautiful "hand off" from his wonderful, never-failing hand of care and guidance to ours.

Humbly sweet and affirming is all well with dad, but that's not all that remains clearly evident of his spirit that would be so familiar to those who know him... Two nights ago he decided he wanted a cup of soup. "Well," I said, "I'm hungry as well. May I join you in a cup of soup?" He looked over at me, gave a great big smile, and said, "Why, yes! Why don't you get in first and then we'll see if there's room for me." He's still got it.

In short, a 'good death' might be understood as a death that directly addresses the needs of the dying person. We have released most of our earlier ideas about how people should die. They only seemed to create more separation and in some cases, even a sense of failure.

At the same time, we hold that people often make the journey from tragedy to transformation if they are properly supported. As caregivers we can hold open possibilities - we can even 'open the door' - but the choice to enter (or not) must always reside with the person who is dying. This appears to involve three key elements:

1. Presence

2. Compassionate Companionship

3. Supportive Inquiry

-from Zen and the Good Death by Frank Ostaseki
(Founding Director: Zen Hospice Project and Founder, Metta Institute)

9... AHHH THE AGITATION

Monday May 19th... it's 3pm and I woke up an hour ago...
the daddy-o team is getting the teaching that most often
accompanies child rearing... it's a good idea to sleep
when he sleeps.
I sat up with him until 2am and then mom pulled the 2- 6
shift and then I went back for the 6 to 9am sitting...
Once again a mal-functioning catheter had him
extra agitated and restless...
we try reading... we try music... we try zanex... and finally
in desperate desire to encourage relief and relaxation
we try morphine... Nuthin'!
It seems he simply needs to be fitful
and to have his fits accommodated.

My impression from others who have walked this path
with a loved one is that it is part of the pattern...
the nurses have warned us (sort of) about it...
And it makes sense to me that this journey would include
a great deal of tension and therefore agitation...
Daddy-o is divided right now... split in two...
he said several days ago "Please put that blanket
on that man's feet" gesturing to his own feet.

He is going through a re-birth... he is in labor...
if he could get up and pace the room
during these active nights I'm sure he would...
oh the frustration!!
to feel the need to move and shuffle...
stretch and expand... and allowed not!
instead bound and swaddled in a body that is breaking
down and no longer granting one's will... Arghhhhh!

And witnessing Daddy-o's struggle
creates the struggle for us, his team…
We cannot fix it.
We cannot wave a magic wand and make it all better.
We just have to sit and watch and fuss around
with warm wash cloths and pillows shifts
or head rubs and gentle chanting...

In between these minor comfort efforts while sitting
I have been doing lots of meditation…
………inhale………
…….exhale…….

Last night it was interesting as I let go
of the thoughts that would arise in my mind…
the "Let Go" became oh so pronounced…
I started seeing our lives as a path of many
mini opportunities to practice letting go
in preparation for death,
our grand and mighty opportunity…

and how we might could shift from dodging and avoiding
-with great emotional expenditure-
these trials we call lose or failure…
and instead embrace them with trust
wrapped in the mystical mantra that "all is well."

Right now all of us Daddy-o fans are faced with such an
opportunity… and of course the trial is greatest for his
beloved wife, Gatra… she has the most to let go of…
a delicate web of energetic weavings
created over their 53 year matrimony…

and to brag a little… she is wearing the mystic
mamma spiritual warrior honorary robe with
stupendous grace and acceptance… which of course
requires nothing less than mammoth strength.
Mamma is rockin' it!
And even more remarkable, she is able to be in
conscious observation of her own letting go practice
while holding space for daddy-o's…
and speak of what she is learning for when it will
be her turn… to move through the tunnel… the
great crossing… the ultimate god trust trial…

Our entire scene is thus hugged by
Mamma's Mountains of Inspiration.

Where 9 days ago we were so sure we only
had a few days left with Daddy-o…
now we know we have no idea!!
And I for one feel so grateful to return my gaze
from the destination back to the journey…
and allow a settling in to it all…
I even wonder if this is part of daddy-o's plan…
the work he is doing now as much for us
and our growth and learning…
as it is for his own.

So we rest in Patience… and Inspiration…
and the softly rocking melody of…
all is well… all is well… all is well.
lovelovelove

10... ELIMINATION

Thursday May 22nd this morning, and really this past week,
the focus for Daddy-o world is all about elimination...
we are back to the basics.

Today he's confused...
at this moment he doesn't remember that he can no
longer get up and walk... and is asking if the bathroom
is available with such an innocent sweetness... as
if somehow he knows he's not supposed to ask but
if he can just say it nicely enough...perhaps.

Oh my gosh... it is heartbreaking to have to
tell my sweet Daddy-o that he can't get up
and go to the toilet anymore!!!!!!!!!!!!!!!

And to his wide-eyed surprise
I try to respond with as much of an
everything's-gonna-be-alright-gaze as I can muster...
hoping to transfer acceptance through our gazes...
But it doesn't work...
My response leaves him looking so downtrodden
it wrenches my gut.

And so I fumble along saying isn't it a funny thing
how god has designed it all...
when we come into this life we are helpless and totally
dependent... our will and choices oh so limited...

also when we are leaving from a place of old age...
when we've been lucky enough to live long...
a natural progression leads us back...
we become again helpless...
dependent upon those around us to care for all we need...

Interesting design choice...
there must be a good reason or god wouldn't
have designed it so... giving us great challenges
based in dependency and very little control
on either side of our lives...
something to contemplate, I said.

Daddy-o wasn't impressed.

And so we are kind of coasting along right now...
bouncing between acceptance and denial...
all the time he is wanting to do what he is supposed to
do... to be the good obedient boy he has always been...
it is all so very precious and endearing.

He is sleeping a lot... less interested in visits...
eating very little bits...
and deeming the Easy Listening radio as
satisfactory entertainment...

We are so grateful to still be at home and able to say that
he is for the most part very comfortable and pain free...
also still super grateful for all the kind attention
and spiritual support y'all are sending!
lovelovelove

The Soul travels;

The body does not travel as much as the soul;

The body has just as great a work as the soul,

and parts away at last for the journeys of the soul.

-Walt Whitman

II… MIRACULOUS WAYS

Tuesday May 27th… Well tomorrow is sweet daddy-o's
87th birthday… I was just sitting with him and Uncle Cole
and Cole was asking Dad if he remembered how old
he was going to be… and it made me ponder… when
did we start counting and celebrating birthdays…?
And why…?
It certainly keeps us very focused on the linear progression
of ourselves and quite frankly probably also keeps us in
constrictive definitions of who and what we are supposed
to be and do according to the observed and celebrated
progression… extra confusing since we celebrate each
year as a small move towards this big looming dread
at the end of the progression…
hummm… very curious design choice, isn't it.

I was actually able to leave daddy-o world this past
weekend and join a small group of beloveds for
some intensely wonderful spiritual retreat work…
The container that held our work is created through
a fusion of several different spiritual traditions…
(one of my favorite things about working with the mystical
teachings is that they are pretty much the same no
matter what religion or tradition has been holding them
over the years… ahhhh… no room for us vs. them!
What a relief, eh?!)

During the weekend I had the space to contemplate some
of the interesting revelations and teachings that have
been delivered throughout the past month's journey with
daddy-o… I thought a lot about christ consciousness and
how it fits into where we are as a human collective right
now in our evolution… and how the death of our physical

form and the struggle and surrender that must come with
it has to be a part of our ascension, our evolution…
that instead of avoiding it we must embrace it…
and celebrate it… and talk about it…
therefore show our trust in our creator god source…
Just think of how our fear and avoidance of death
must frustrate god!…
that we would hold doubt in our hearts that our dear
unconditionally loving creator god would give us some
horrific nightmare of an exit… some final doom…
I do not see christ in this picture…

The avoidance of struggle and surrender is what creates
the fertile ground for the seeds of suffering to germinate…
being present to the struggle and surrender with complete
acceptance leaves no room for suffering… si o no..?
Daddy-o was in a place of acceptance the first four
or five days or so… We were traveling between the
worlds and the challenges were stimulating…
My first post went out on that Monday and on Tuesday
he received around 50 visitors… He wanted me by his
side all day during the deluge of love and attention…
At that time my ego was fluffed up for I was thinking
"aww, I'm daddy-o's warrior angel and he needs
my strength and experience next to him."
Not!
This weekend I saw the truth…
He wanted me to watch his mastery so that I might learn…
There he was… totally out there… straddling the veils…
vibrating at an incredible place of acceptance and love…
so close to god…
and even while hovering in this other-worldly out there
godhood kind of space… daddy-o was able to meet
each visitor where they were at… at their level…
with unwavering presence and compassion…

30

all the while never shifting his own expanded vibration…
giving giving giving…
now that's a christ consciousness kinda thang!
if'n you ask me ;-)…

When I returned from my spiritual retreat the daddy-o
team reported one restless fitful night… though now
he is mostly sleeping. When he wakes up he is usually
confused as to why and where… time to get up and
go do something… or why am I in this hotel…?
what is swaddled around me…? such things.
A few times he has really insisted on knowing what is
going on with him…when he does I say… "your soul is
being called over to god and your body is dying so that
it can go." I don't know if it is the right thing to say…
I just know that is what I would want to hear.

Daddy-o's journey is somewhat special for these modern
times… he doesn't have some terminal illness…
we can't remind him of his diagnosis…
it truly is a vision of being called…
or maybe just good ol' Old Age.

Tomorrow immediate family will gather around
to celebrate daddy-o with some of his favorite dishes…
salmon, cheese grits, asparagus,
chocolate cake and ice cream….
We continue to marvel and be amazed by him
and how he is working it all…
as he continues teaching us in miraculous ways…
Grateful for each day!!
lovelovelove

12... THE BEST CALL OF ALL

Thursday may 30th... feeling summertime's warm
approach as i swim in a reflective pool...
my thoughts swirling around...
if i am not careful they may pull me under...
but then that might be alright... sinking into
the depths of dreamy watery illusion...
it is so tempting as the temperatures rise...

i do believe daddy-o feels the temptation as well...
last night he was swirling in song....
our oh-so-simple tune that frames birthday tradition...
he began requesting it right away...
"but everyone's not here yet" gatra said...
"that's okay we can sing it again"...
and we did... as he requested it over and over...

perhaps it was the most comfortable way
for him to connect with the group...
perhaps he was acknowledging that it would be the last
time bill mallard would be the name sung in this simple
familiar melody giving step to our earthly march...
"oh me"...

yesterday morning daddy-o was "grumpy"...
not a word often associated with this man's character...
and i felt him...

his need that day to somehow perform as the center of attention when he did not know "how to present himself"... he asked us this question "how do i present myself for my birthday?"...

and we did not have an adequate answer...
to continue lying in bed...?
how could that ever be adequate...? to give some speech about how it feels... lying in bed dying and at the same time celebrating your birthday...? whoa!

I don't know daddy-o... I'm so sorry i don't have a good answer... please forgive me.

and so the journey continues... for me it is a constant pounding upon my heart and mind to align myself to love and trust... to wrap myself in a bubble that gives allowance... an allowance that says daddy-o has received a call... a call he must answer... a good call... a wonderful call... the best call of all...

and the best love i can show him is by shifting little by little in correspondence to his shifts...
to be as conscious as i possibly can in each now moment...
as he is letting go... i am letting go...
subtle energetic cords to reconfigure...
as he rewires so must i...
it's only fair!
lovelovelove

Make the place as beautiful as possible;
a calm, peaceful, serene, holy environment is so important.
There should be beautiful views, beautiful art, flowers,
images of deities and holy beings.
The point is to make a positive imprint on the person's mind.
The person's mind is elevated and they are not afraid of dying.

– Lama Zopa Rinpoche
(Tibetan Buddhist Scholar and Founder of the Foundation
for the Preservation of the Mahayana Tradition)
Used with permission from FPMT Inc. www.fpmt.org

13... THE WATCH AND GATRA

Saturday morning the last day of may..."oh me"...
i have indulged in a second cafe-mocha this morning as
i sit in the corner coffee shop... i suppose i am trying to
resist this haze... to give lift to this droopy heavy curtain
that has been hanging about my shoulders the past day
or two...i wouldn't go so far as to call it depression...
but perhaps a spiritual recession...
or maybe just an empathetic connection
to where daddy-o is hovering...
whatever it is the coffee really isn't making
a difference... tastes good though...
an indulgence for indulgence's sake perhaps...

Daddy-o has never really been drawn to such
indulgences... he has always been a man of gentle
discipline and relaxed yet committed schedule...
and still is today...

after rising from my bed i went in to sit next to his...
he asked me how the day looked...?
I said "well I see some sparkly golden light that looks as if
it has possibility of expanding into a bright sunny day"...
he said "ahhh how nice... sparkles expanding...
and what is your outlook for this day...?"...
I responded and asked him if he had a nice outlook for
this day as well... he said "well I need to work on that"...
then he hollered for Gatra... his guide for said outlook...
she was busy but would be in in a minute...
he said to me that whatever his outlook was it
involved her so he had to consult with her...

After mom came in, the consult determined that it
would be good to go ahead and get him cleaned up
and turned so that he could rest on his side…
the hospice team taught us that to protect his backside
from getting sores we need to have him resting on one side
then the other for at least 2 hours per side each day…
Once adjusted and on his side
(he is always preciously cooperative
when we have to "mess with him" in such ways)
he asked about the schedule…
"now how long am I supposed to be like this…?"
I said "well our goal daddy-o is two hours… if you get
uncomfortable though we can turn back sooner"…

I went and did things and returned about
30 mins later and he said …
"well I think it is time for me to move along with my day…
I think I am done here"…
I told him that actually if he could stay there for a while
longer it would be good… he needed this confirmed with
Gatra of course… and so she went into the room and said
yes if he could stay on his side a while longer it would be
good… then 5 mins later he was calling for me… he wanted
to let me know that he thought he was done now…

in this moment I realized what he needed was
a precise time that was the end goal…
so i said well Daddy-o we shifted you to your side a little after
9am so if you could be here until 11am – which is another 1
hour and 10 mins… that would be the ultimate goal… as soon
as he had the 11am time goal in his mind things got better….
a peaceful resolve entered the scenario...

he has not taken his watch off and checks it often...
even when he is quite out of it he will lift his arm
out of habit to look at it...
just giving himself the accustomed action of lift
and turn orienting watch face to head tilt...
face to face he receives the gesture of schedule...
the motion of routine...
the glance that tells him how he is coming along
with that day's outlook...

The watch and Gatra...
they are his two anchors right now...
or the two staffs holding him up...
or his two advisers with whom he sits in counsel
determining the next appropriate move...
so many ways of viewing it...
certainly they are the two things he has used the
longest to hold his life and reality together...
his schedule and his beloved wife...
and so in keeping they seem to be the two things
that will be the hardest for him to let go of...
of course...

and so the struggle and the joy...
the confusion and the clarity... the wonder and the murk...
are all still informing each day... each moment...
as we carry on...
feeling each of you with us...
circling round and round
within this dreamy sacred wheel...
with gratitude always!
lovelovelove

On Earth there's a lot of who's-better-than-who type issues

and that causes a lot of suffering.

It's a game devised by the forces of Maya, or illusion,

to make people unhappy.

That's one of the purposes of illusion: human misery.

-The Afterlife of Billy Fingers by annie kagan

14... COLEMAN'S NEW MOON

Monday june 2... well... wondering how to let my
heart open and share... here and now...
as my feelings are soaking in hurt and sadness...
waves of realization carry me into and outoff
the acknowledgement that Coleman Lewis and I
will never again hang out in the backyard...
talking and crying about the curses and the blessings...
struggles and delights...
he was so in tune to the melody of human life...
perhaps in some ways too in tune.

Recently we were trying to figure a recovery plan
that might fit his style.
And i must say that was a challenge to envision because
so much of what "recovery" entailed just wasn't
coleminer's style...
to look at him and see all the re-patterning
and re-wiring needed...
i said to him once "coleman we need a rotorooter
for your energy body/spirit"...

my thought was if i could just get him to peru...
maybe with the help of jungle magic...
but when it came down to it, before peruvian medicine
could be a possible portal, there were some tough
rough currents he needed to swim through...
he would have to work hard... recovery = hard work...
no matter what twist we put on it...
and coleman just wasn't put on this planet
to be a worker-bee...

he was put on this planet to be a lover... a jester...
a maker of dark beauty...
and that is good... and he fulfilled this goodness...
his calling.

our culture is really mean to the lovers...
it tells us we are not adequate... we are too sensitive...
not following the rules of responsibility and so forth...

A cesspool of judgement is the united states of today...
and when we are carrying on to function and live in
a stinky cesspool the survival mode becomes
masks and distractions...
these are our addictions…
and anyone who has some lover left in them
will have moments if not daily use...

When we have judgments as to how and when
sweet coleminer left us...
we are feeding the cesspool...
and therefore the culture of addiction...

Coleman is a truly compassionate being.
Though i know he saw them all, he rarely showed me my
foibles... and when he did it was with complete acceptance
and forgiveness... in this way he is my teacher...
and my gratitude and love are eternal.
yes he has left us and his beloved son, dury, and
we can be angry about that... for a minute... but to
linger there... no... it feeds the wrong world...

the world we want dury to know is the one he had
with his dad... sweet light fun vulnerability
snuggled within compassionate acceptance... and trust...
trust that coleman's life and death was divinely perfect...
and trust that this loss is an important part of dury's
sacred walk... one that will give him the strength
and wisdom he needs for his mission here...

to allow and honor each person's mission and path as
just right for them is an important ingredient in all of
us moving beyond our addictions and dis-ease...
how we re-wire this culture of judgment...
filter and clean the cesspool.

Coleman did and is still doing his part... thanks coleminer!!
love you soooooo much sweet brother!

daddy-o expressed frustration that he could only be
a part of the Lewis family sadness from a distance...
he very much is aware of what has happened... and
wishes he could "get out of this box" and be more
attentive and helpful... he loved coleman too... and
treasures the precious neighborly connection the
mallards and the lewis' have always maintained...

and soon he will be swimming with coleman
in an awareness far greater
than anything us left behind
are able to understand...
that is until we catch up with them...
lovelovelove

15... NUTHIN LEFT TO DO BUT GROW GROW GROW

June 6... it feels a little risky to think of writing right now...
i feel pretty wide open and filterless...
i've hardly slept... my brain has shrunk...
and my heart is as fat as fat can be...

Daddy-o said to me this morning... "well i'm trying to
make sense of this position i've gotten myself into"...
With a deep breath i suggested
and he thought it was a good idea that he use his
heart instead of his head to try and make sense of it...
our mind can just confuse us when we try to use it
to make sense of certain things...
many things...

7 nights ago a portal opened... a juxtaposition
skewed the curtain... dissolve was commanded...
dissolve beyond earthairfirewater...
mystical moment striking lightning flash...
silent potent dissolve... and poof!
coleman's gone...

but not totally... because i've been riding
a heartmagic carpet with him since then...
and the ride has been remarkable...
it's been in my breath... or hanging out on the other
side of my breath... looking in... looking in at winn...
the character the ego the conditions the motions...
my simple careless thoughts over there...
feelings too... over there... they seem different...
my eyes have changed...? no... i'm just perched
in a new view... coleman is holding me...

42

i'm sitting in his hand... and the outlook... well... dissolve...
a long dark moonless night... spreading... dissolving...
into the blanket of stars...
high light density...
every cell a star...
breathe in breathe out… my cells...
milkyway of vital love...
here in coleman's hand i know...
i am... vital love... truth...
i am...

i pray to know this place... to remember...
as the days stroll on... as i wake from the suffering joy
of this precious catastrophe...
coleman!! your hand feels so good... please hold me...
as long as you can... your dissolve is my champion...
i need it... you... i need you... just exactly as you are...
so i might be different... better... a clearer view of truth...
my voice my song... your dissolve the perfect tuning...
dancing rocking my essence... my share... my love...
my life...
you hold me... i hold you... eternity is our show...
might as well make it a hip shake thang...si o no?...
cause nuthin left to do but grow grow grow!

the first thing claire, coleman's sis, said to me was…
"just in case you needed a little more death in your life"...
and yes… but also just in case i needed a little
more mystical experience in my life...
rich scrumptious aliveness is the death struggle...
with deep respect and honor i give thanks...
lovelovelove

16... CURTAINS OF THE BEYOND

monday june 9th - ooowee how could that be...
the days are traveling swiftly it seems...
I walked into daddy-o's room around 1:30 today with a
towel on my head just out of the shower and he said
"i'm glad to see you are generously wrapped up
in the curtains of the beyond..."

I love his way of seeing things...mixing things...
i was just getting up for the day as I had sat with him
all night... we have moved back into the more active
"labor" style mode... on this past friday his catheter
messed up again and so sistah-morphine was
brought in to work her magic which included a hazy
afternoon in and out with mumbled ramblings...
and one clear declaration repeated several times –
"time to get this celebration back on me."

Yes daddy-o you are right... it is time...
so then Sunday, yesterday morning, we saw that he had
indeed made a shift back towards how it had been
the first week of may...
maybe moving from denial towards acceptance...?
or from a resting moment back into the work, the labor...?
or relying less on the ego
and moving more towards soul being...?
so many ways to think and look at it...

definitely the pull between staying and going
more pronounced...
the place of earthbound vs godbound pulling at him...
oh sweet daddy-o...

the "oh me's" are returning... the hiccups too...
perhaps for only a moment… perhaps longer...
experience tells us there's no telling.

sunday morning began with a wonderful conversation
between daddy-o, mom and myself...
he was wanting to bargain...
even though our apartment is one floor... he was
saying he is upstairs and we are all downstairs
and he's wondering if we can keep the same rhythm
of the "whirlygig" (ceiling fan)
but just move him downstairs...
he asked gatra "can we be on the same floor please
and keep things between us... in the same rhythm...?"

gatra responded that they are going to have to be
on different floors but will always be in the
"same space... or same universe... or same love."
dad liked "the same love" the best...
"we will use this... the same love...
winndy - mom and i want to be in the same love...
what do you think of this..?"
"i think it sounds perfect daddy-o."
And so he declared
"That we can be in the same love and lo it is done!"

After a long pause he said "we need to have our
ranks closed right."... and then moments later asked...
"can we find a place of peace and understanding and
much good will with no loss of strength of will...?"
I said sounds great can you teach us how...?
He said "I think that showing participants what needs to
happen is part and parcel of who we are and what we do."

And so it is and so we are...
cuddled up in the smiles and tears...
while witnessing and allowing the struggle...
his struggle stretching betwixt earth and god...
our struggle trusting that we can be in the same love
and lo it is done.

coleman was with us last night
through the wee morning hours...
in small moments dad was talking to some being
out there... over there...
and i couldn't help but sense it to be coleman...
waiting in the same love...
patient and kind guidance
as a semi-permeable membrane...
waiting to help carry daddy-o once he is ready.

grateful as always to be in the same love with all of you...
feeling the treasure of community so deeply...
lovelovelove

At death, the thing that casts the shadow
withdraws, and metabolism ceases.
Material form breaks down; it ceases to be a dissipative structure
in a very localized area, sustained against
entropy by cycling material in,
extracting energy, and expelling waste.
But the form that ordered it is not affected.

These declarative statements are made from the point of view
of the shamanic tradition, which touches all higher religions.
Both the psychedelic dream state and the waking psychedelic state
acquire great import because they reveal to life a task,
to become familiar with this dimension that is causing being,
in order to be familiar with it at the moment of passing from life.

- Terence McKenna
from "A talk given at the invitation of Ruth and Arthur Young of
the Berkeley Institute for the Study of Consciousness" (1984)
collected in The Archaic Revival (1991)

17... FOLLOWING THE MOON

full moon friday the thirteenth... oohlala...
feeling the jazzy sexy sassy thang today as i allow
the precious synchronicity of feminine energy
to sweep me off my feet a wee bit...

13 the number of the goddess for there are 13 moons
and she is the holder of receptivity...
receiving the light of her lover, the majestic sun…
and reflecting his power with gentle filtered beauty...
Marvel!…
to be able to receive and reflect in such a way...
no room for taking...
floating as a lake of pure potential…
patiently awaiting conscious and direct attention...
receiving the focus...
and in that instant... within that magical interface...
the spark of creation ignites new light... new life...
new being...
'a' met 'h' and they said aaaahhhhh...
deliciously satisfying... indeed.

last night i went to a friend's house to dance
into some of my full moon jitters...
when i returned i heard mom and dad in their room
talking... apparently dad had been asking over and
over about the time and what it meant for him...
mom was saying "it's 1am sweetheart
and it means it's time to sleep..."

as i walked in daddy-o lit up...
eyes wide and voice expanded... he said
"oh looky who's here... my guide and friend...
look dear who is here... our guide and friend!
What do you say guide and friend about what time it is...?"
I can't remember exactly what i said
but something about the full moon shining brightly
and that i was letting her be my guide...
daddy-o said "well then i will follow you and the moon...
yes you and the moon will be my guides"
oh my goddess!... could an adoring daughter ever ask
for more of an affirmation from her beloved father...?!

daddy-o's magical brilliance is completely intact if not even
enhanced by this sacred journey... all week he has been
hanging out... bouncing between... earth and god...
and he's mostly been extremely upbeat...
positive in his expressions...
i might even go so far as to say the vibe has
mostly been one of joyful acceptance!!
we have had to explain and remind him
now and again what is going on...
"tell me again why i am in this box"...
and he's had wonderful replies like
"don't give me that spiritual mumbojumbo"
or
"well if i get the call and have to leave I just want you
both to know that i love you dearly."... with no sadness..
or sappy remorse... just very matter of fact.

Wednesday morning he was more actively interested regarding the hospice aide coming that day to wash him up... he said to gatra... "prepare for the cleaning crew that is coming... stay in bed and let it wash over me... be like a shiny new penny. I am not put off by these realities. Take care to clean up, lie here and let them do it. Take things as they come...that covers it."

In the 2 am drowsy that night he and gatra had another wonderful exchange where his "mind understood and it felt like a dark and forbidding place"... so he set out to light christmas lights!!... then he realized he was lost... "so give up my foolish search until daylight comes and i have some possibility... the people i was with will understand i was lost... i will begin search again when conditions are favorable." oh my daddy-o!!

and so i sit as still and patient as i can... open to receive and reflect... the brilliance of this man... shining like a shiny new penny... big-smile wide-eyes... arms thrown up into the air... riding his destiny... his calling... his sacred spiritual rollercoaster...

with each breath i feel unspeakable gratitude and honor... and in my utopian idealized world every daughter and every son on the planet will have their own moment to receive... reflect... and thus expand... into an even more brilliant version of divine humanness... i mean we might as well, right?... yeah!... daddy-o says "Go For It!" lovelovelove

18... RAZOR'S EDGE

feeling deeply the moon waves...
as sweet <u>Coleman</u> ripped my heart open 2 weeks ago...
sneaking out...
sliding down the razors edge without a whisper...
covered and wrapped
in the deep black dark moon blanket...

now here i sit... still askew and amiss...
in the full moon glow... so different as she shines brilliant
with complete confidence and exuberance...
the honey moon they call her... of course! how perfect!
cause coleman was a honey...
golden glow you are... sweet honey love of mine...

his nickname in our band, *lip-lock-alarm-clock*,
was "sweet sticky thang"...

and all in keeping for coleman was a moon child...
he knew the wax and wane of this game
we call being human on planet earth...
the empty and the full...
supa-star spot light full moon nights
of satisfaction and glory...
on the heels of how low and dark can we go...
he knew dynamics! he felt all of them deeply...
he couldn't do superficial... anything.

and now he is up there.. out there... over there...
and you know i'm figurin' he's gettin' to skip some
of the more cumbersome levels or stages
(or what have you)
within the whole after-life gauntlet...
cause coleman didn't have very many attachments
to things or beliefs...
not a whole lot of earthly goo to let go of...

he was a free bird...
riding the moon waves... allowing the dynamic slopes
to lift him up... and drop him back down...
bang! ouch! he had some hard falls!...
but maybe that's okay cause the dynamics kept him light –
can't ride the waves with heavy luggage...
so now he's reapin' the benefits...
flyin' high and easy in angel land...
what's that expression –
"angels can fly cause they take themselves so lightly"
like that...

though because he did have one big attachment...
i reckon he's flowin' in currents
that aren't too far off coast...
cause myohmy did he love his son, dury!...
so he's drifting with one eye locked in
on that little buddy... for sure... for now...

love you coleminer...
sweet honey moon dark angel friend love of mine...
holding you hugging you feeling you!!!

For when we travel between the worlds, we can change all the worlds.

And in both of our worlds healing can occur.

So we stand here on the shore of the Sunless Sea of our tears and grief,

and with our courage, our need, and our love,

we travel to meet our beloved dead.

-The Pagan Book of Living and Dying:
Practical Rituals, Prayers, Blessings, and Meditations on Crossing Over
by Starhawk and M. Macha Nightmare & The Reclaiming Collective

19... BEYOND THE OLD ROLES

It's father's day and as i was shaving daddy-o this morning
- usually an activity for reid or rob –
i was thinking about the intimacy of it all...
as the roles we have worn all these years change or fall
away... as the filters and acceptable interactions shift...
a whole new level of intimacy is made possible...
we can choose to be really present and thus
allow the intimacy to enter... really feel it...
or we can dodge it... perhaps adopting other roles
like "care-taker and patient"... Or we can switch
roles – he's the child I'm the parent... Sounds less
than ideal to me, doesn't it?... let's not go there!
so to be present and connect beyond the old roles...
take off the masks...
i mean that is what daddy-o is having to do...
let go of his old roles...
take off the professor's robe... release the mallard humor...
give up his routine...
exit the stage that defines him in relation to other
humans... husband and father... uncle and brother...
he cannot take these character aspects with him, and
quite frankly he just doesn't have the energy right now...
maybe that's why he is sleeping so much...
to keep up with the role playing at this point takes
a lot of his energy...
and I do not at all mean to imply that any aspect
of daddy-o has not been genuine...
to the contrary
he developed and wore his personality/character
garb with great enthusiasm and authenticity...
and has worn them oh-so-well...

it is just what we do when we incarnate as human
on planet earth... we take on personality roles
that encase our soul essence... right...?
and as he is sort of practicing leaving...
plus functioning on less energy...
he is having moments where he is not being a role...
and when I have been able to meet him
without playing my role as daughter...
in those rare and precious moments...
we have together evolved to a new level of connection...
we have shared true spiritual intimacy...
where we have met soul to soul...
not role to role...

these moments have been terrifying and miraculous!!

and I marvel at the miracle with unspeakable gratitude...
while acknowledging the kooky unorthodox path
I have walked so far in this world...
with its accompanying struggles and heartaches...
I wouldn't trade one millisecond...
because the teachings and lessons have afforded me
this gift... this divine blessing...
soul to soul...

the next day – monday june 16... didn't finish
yesterday... and in contrast to the soul to soul thang
we did have a wonderful family gathering
celebrating the role to role thang...
father and grandfather...

reid and rob and their families came over
and we ate daddy-o's favorites –
salmon, spicy spinach and cheese grits…
reid's wife, alison, had the honor of assisting daddy-o
with his meal and I think she went back three times to
get more… he hasn't eaten that much in quite a while!
We circled around him and read or spoke
words of recognition and gratitude…
we reminisced about fun family moments as well as some
hard or tragic moments… he received it all beautifully…
fully participating and enjoying the attention…
it was a super sweet celebration!

and today he seems different from how he
was last week… a bit more confused…
he said "winndy… I think I've been in bed all morning"…
I said "yes well…" and he interjected
"well that seems very lazy!"

death is super real… it's nitty gritty…
there just ain't no way to paint it pretty or sugar coat it…
but by goodness!, i'm gonna look and find the treasures
that are buried within the murk…
and to do that I gotta go into the murk… eeek!
"feel the fear and do it anyway… feel the fear
and do it anyway" I say to myself…

one of the scary treasures… soul to soul…
letting go of roles…
perhaps we fear this level of intimacy
as much as we do death itself…
as daddy-o says "I'll ponder this"…
lovelovelove

20… LABOR

wednesday june 25th...jeez this month has flown!!
here we are - back into it...
i left town for 6 nights to take care of other personal
stuff... and during that time sweet daddy-o had some
more catheter trauma which resulted in an infection
and a swing back into what i have been calling "labor"...
once again he's out there!... trippin'!!...
very similar to the first week starting may 5th...
it's altered state...
it's labor...
the re-birthing process in full swing...
now he might come back from it and rest another while
in a place of earth and murk...
or this time he might let the chariot carry him home...
we are sure not to try and predict anything with this
man anymore!... he definitely has his own ideas and
ways of working his program... and we love this!!

i sat up with him all night last night...
gently rubbing his arm or chest or head
to help alleviate the hiccups...
while he was busy all night with thoughts and
encounters... i was fighting my own delirium thinking
that he was offering me a window into that world...
this world... the place in between...

it made me think about what i must have been doing
as a wee human growing and developing inside mother
and then the moments before plopping out
into the official winn mallard role...

we go through an altered state of consciousness...
when entering and leaving this dimension – i reckon...
and i wonder how similar they are...?

today he had the sensation of falling again...
my spiritual teacher, Carol E Parrish-Harra, advised me
"If you get a chance tell him to pretend he is floating on his
back in a swimming pool. This is the sensation one feels
as they are going into the astral and leaving their body."

"daddy-o... just float on your back like it is water"...
just right now instead of water
it's the world of energy...?
god...?
the ascended beings and angels...?
ancestors...?
or all of the above...
yeh... something... he obviously knows quite a few
entities over there... wherever... whoever they are...
he seems quite comfortable with them...
one was even a bright ball of orange light that he
kept seeing and saying it had messages...
"did you get that, winndy...?"
"sorry dad... i'm not quite there... wish i was"...

my time will come soon enough...
and thank the heavens for this teacher!...
my sweet daddy-o... showing me how
i might experience conscious death one day...
with a pinch of luck and grace and good living...
i can only hope...
lovelovelove

The disciples said to Jesus, "Tell us, how will our end come?"

Jesus said, "Have you found the beginning,

then, that you are looking for the end?

You see, the end will be where the beginning is.

Congratulations to the one who stands at the beginning:

that one will know the end and will not taste death."

-Gospel of Thomas, logion 18 The Gnostic Society Library,

translated by Stephen Patterson and Marvin Meyer

21... THE OTHER END OF
THE ICE CREAM

Remembering <u>Coleman</u> today, friday june 26th...
as it is the next new moon... a dark cloak wrapping him...
wrapping us... 1 month mark and it is still so dreamy and
surreal... did he really go...? indeed... he's not here
but he's not far either... love you coleman!

Daddy-o on the other hand seems to be back!
after several nights of no sleep and much traveling... he
and therefore we... slept through the night last night and he
has been asleep all day as well... he is no longer roaming
the range of other dimensions... he is here and present and
wanting to get out of bed so that he can give gatra a big hug...

And journeying with him was delightful!...
One of the nights while i was sitting up with him he was
in some small southern town giving the program at the
local church... (something he did manymany times)...
i walked into the room and he gave me a big smile
introducing himself and extending his hand for a shake...
"I'm bill mallard" he said in a light blissful tone...
i said "pleased to meet you"...
"thank you" he replied... "now i wonder if you can
help me... i can't seem to find my cell phone
and i have a program to give at 5 o'clock..."
we carried on for hours with this little vignette...
during it all he was so enthusiastically full of genuine
delight to be an honored guest in the little town...
excited that he might bring some joy and inspiration
to the group who was awaiting his arrival...

i had always known daddy-o on either side of these
"teaching ventures"... leaving and returning... and so for
the first time ever i was actually with him - a little bit –
on one of his wee pilgrimages exploring the depths of
the deep south through its small sweet church groups...
spreading the light through song and laughter framed
in his unique and enlightened way of sharing
the new testament... the new creation.
i am so glad...
a different glimpse of daddy-o... yet another gift!...

and what a fun breath of fresh air he must've
been in these often overlooked… possibly
stagnant and humid dots on the map...
and oh my how he obviously enjoyed bringing joy!
and connecting with all kind of folk...
one of daddy-o's greatest abilities - to connect genuinely
with all different kinds of people... from the super intellectual
super fancy to the super meek super simple... he never cast
judgment as to anyone being better or lesser... and everyone
could feel his acceptance and love no matter who they were...
perhaps his most remarkable quality and teaching for me.

during these days of "dimensional exploration"
we had a pad of paper next to his bed so we might
capture some of his amazing musings...
something he said on tuesday while reid was sitting with
him – "i'm going on to glory." - pause - "Pray on Pray on"
- pause - "the jig is up... i will be exploring the new...
i don't want to go without acknowledging the human
power... we seem to have made a turn!"
go daddy-o go!! go human power go!!

another thing he said while gatra was sitting with him...
"here is the other end of the ice cream...
i gander and learn to wonder again"...

such beautiful precious moments!!

and just to give a status style update
in response to some of your questions...
even though he hasn't left the bed since may 5th...
daddy-o is pain free and very comfortable here at
home... our only issue has been the catheter which
is necessary or his bladder wont empty... it has
taken us a while to get the maintenance down...
(i will write a catheter maintenance manual as the hospital
makes a mistake sending folk home with little or no info)...

He is drug free except when we have to change the
catheter and then receives a small dose of morphine...
He is not dying of any particular disease...
he said to gatra back in January
"i feel like the life force is draining out of me"...
and said to me when i arrived in march "well
winndy, i think the role of bill mallard is over but
i've had so much fun i don't want it to end"...

so it is all as good as it can get! remarkable really...
and all of you and your prayers and wishes are a gigantic
part of the remarkableness... community matters!
tribe elevates us beyond...
the whole is greater than the sum of its parts...
always with outstanding gratitude!
lovelovelove

Throughout his life, Yeshua continued to choose

to step into the true kingdom of his "I AM"

until every cell in his body knew and accepted union with its Creator.

In this simple, direct way, Yeshua simultaneously passed

through crucifixion, resurrection, and ascension,

and so can you!

-Anna, Grandmother of Jesus by Claire Heartsong

22... ELDEST SON'S 50TH

tuesday... sort of just a normal uneventful tuesday...
though it is july 1st... which means...
that <u>Reid</u>'s 50th birthday is tomorrow... Yeah Reid!

It also means that we might be facing our first "family
event" that won't be at mom and dad's place and sweet
daddy-o wont be able to attend... that's big actually...
he's missing his first "family celebration"... perhaps ever!!

mama had been remembering recently... how daddy-o had
been the chair of graduate studies back in 1970 or so...
i was 5 years old and in mrs boozer's dance/theater
class that she held in her converted garage at her
home on houston mill road... i remember we would do
fun simple dance moves as we crisscrossed through
the space... practicing singing and voice projection
good ol' theatrical expression - "being dramatic"...
during our little class we would work towards a final
recital or performance... which included little costumes
where we were mice and flowers and fairies and such...
dancing and singing... our wings lifting us into wee
pirouettes and our petals splaying out as we twirled into
dizzy wonder... all the while being ecstatically dramatic...

"good grief!" - one of daddy-o's favorite expressions –
and probably what he said when he heard that my
grand finale performance recital was the same
night as his graduate seminar!... "good grief!"
and seein' how he was the chair of said seminar
it was not exactly something he could skip...

any of you who have functioned within the ivory tower
of academia know that there can be great pressure and
expectation placed upon professors -especially younger
ones- to prioritize their professorly duties before all else...
but daddy-o resisted this pressure and simply changed
the date of the seminar -never mind putting folk out–
so he could watch his daughter dressed up as a daisy...
twirl and fumble her way across stage...

mama was recalling this memory as an "indication of dad's
priority of being present at the children's activities"...
home every night by 6:30 for our family dinner even
though he always returned to work afterwards...
getting awards for the most enthusiastic cheerleader
at our soccer games (one funny british ref turned
to me not realizing he was my dad and said, "my
god, who is that foghorn on the sidelines..?!")...
and applauding and cheering at our recitals and often
wacky musical theater events which have continued
basically until this day... and, of course, always
always present at any life event celebration...
with bells on and usually a delightful home-made card!

And now he can't be there... his body won't let him...
and so we have to decide do we even tell
him a celebration is happening...?
and then we have to adjust to the empty space
that will be oh so obvious as we gather without him...

so feeling the sadness of this other letting go...
even though my spiritual gifts and experiences show me
he will always be present – just in a less obvious form...

i will miss what his body and personality brought...
in the moment... at the event...
his laughter filling the sometimes awkward moments...
holding his hand to circle up and give thanks...
his gentle sacred blessings hugging us and the all...
the original and rare daddy-o sweetness coating the
scene... assisting everyone in feeling a little more love.

on a more logistical note... we continue to learn... one
major thing is being careful about the food he eats... most
specifically after coming off of one of his "labor phases"
where he eats very very little... either the amount of
food or the cheesiness of his choices - or both - seems
to have caused acid re-flux which oddly appears as
congestion... lots of coughing and his ears stopped up...
these symptoms on top of continued mild hiccups were
pounding on him for several days... in response he was
more needy and restless than usual... but of course.

and yesterday carol, the hospice nurse, declared his lungs
to be fine... we also moved to nice brothy soups and fresh
squeezed arden's garden juices as a hopeful remedy...
which seem to have helped... for last night he slept
soundly with no coughing or hiccups! yeeeeeedawgie!
oh sweet daddy-o you will be missed by so many so
deeply... but most especially by us - the daddy-o team...
for even when you're needy you are still a joy!

so we are resting in the joy and the sadness
and sending both out to all of you...
the dualism of human wonder!
incredible isn't it!
lovelovelove

Because of our multiplicity,

we can consciously move between differing realms of existence.

We are a particle fixed in the space/time

but also a unity of consciousness beyond time or space.

The gift we receive from our multiple levels of perception is

that as quantum beings we can finally understand

that separation is an illusion.

We can begin to perceive that we are part of an ever-expanding whole

and that the entire universe may itself be

an immeasurable hologram that some call God.

-Return of the Children of Light;
Incan and Mayan Prophecies for a New World
by Judith Bluestone Polich

23... A GENTLE BREEZE BLOWING THAT CAN SHIFT THE ENTIRE WORLD

Tuesday July 8th.... sweet daddy-o was very focused on
the door last night as he has been from time to time...
he was saying "now out there beyond that door is a
network... a network with different locations"...
indeed, i thought.
Since he hasn't left the bed since may 5th his material
world has existed only of this small bedroom
- his bed facing the door that enters into the living room
thus this door front and center in his view...
the hospital bed, compliments of hospice,
provides a minuscule change in perspective
as it raises his head up and down...
otherwise he is truly limited regarding stimulus
via the physical sphere...
the door, the ceiling fan and the items that are
situated on the dresser to the left of the door.

mama and i have been reading a fascinating and
uplifting book called *the afterlife of billy fingers*...
as i was sitting next to daddy-o's bed reading it i thought
to ask him what his ideas or beliefs were about the
afterlife... his response was wonderfully reflective
of his current reality...
he said something about it is "full of symbols and signs...
for example much like the door and the ceiling fan."
I love the way he makes the best of his limited situation!

Of course, the important ingredients which instantly
expand his world are visits from beloveds... as soon
as a loved one walks into the room he is animated and
illuminated with enthusiastic interest and gratitude...
most of the time that is.
There have been moments where visits have felt
overwhelming and he has let us know and we
do our best to keep things quiet and easy...
the waves and dimensions of this journey being far
more vast than his small simple confinement.

He keeps the daddy-o team on our toes...
especially with the subtleties of the transition...
a gentle breeze barely blowing that can shift
the entire world.

Coleman is also a subtle yet constant companion
in my daddy-o love story...
as dad was paying note to the network beyond the door
i was seeing coleman in one of those other locations...
and it occurred to me that instead of re-membering coleman
as he was... pulling on memories from my mind...
it felt much better to re-know coleman
in his new formless form...
to go beyond my mind...
to rest in the present moment instead of past moments...
and open my heart and being to
a new way of connecting with him...
one that might lead to
a whole other level of intimate trust...

changing my perspective
and therefore offering me a door...
a portal to a new understanding...
a glimpse into the mystery...
while at the same time perhaps encouraging
coleman's journey instead of pulling on him...

And then, of course, all these thoughts shifted to sweet
daddy-o and how i can begin to do the same with him...
to be as conscious as i can
and in the present moment when i am with him...
one great benefit being that then i am much more likely
to notice the subtle shifts...
but also so i can transition as he is...
so i can be completely open
to re-knowing him as he changes...
encouraging his transition with a confidence
that it is right and beautiful...
holding him without holding him back...

perhaps this is the greatest love challenge
we face in all of our relationships...
while we are standing in our physical forms certainly...
and so in keeping as we make our grand transitions...
holding without holding back... "oh me!"

and so the gratitude and awakenings continue...
ever flowing flowing...
from our center of being and wondering to yours...
gentle precious intimate love.
lovelovelove

24... HALLELUJAH PIE IN
A CRUST OF TRUST

monday mid-day july 14th.... well perhaps i have grounded
a little bit... i've been floating in a mixed bubble
of intense sorrow and joy since friday night's rehearsal
for Coleman's sat afternoon memorial service...
floating flying crying smiling... feeling... feeling deeply...
allowing the feelings to take me
and do with me as they will (for the most part anyway...)
hallehlujah!!
such a great word... and it is.. he is... coleman...
daddy-o... all of us... we all are hallelujah!...
hallelujah pie in a crust of trust!

needless to say the memorial service was
stunning and exquisite... the best part was its
authenticity and truth *sweetly - gently - held*
by accountability and responsibility...

And then there were the Colors! - well! "oh my!"...
bright gorgeous scrumptious colors and flavors
of music and poetry and personalities
creating ceremonial art at its best! by goddess!!...
divinely crafted in perfect coleman style
- effortless and real.

when i returned home to daddy-o's side after the
festivities it was 1am and he was wild and wired!
(uncle cole came down from virginia to sit with him
so mama and i could be free to be present
with the lewis family)...
and i dare say the euphoric emotional bubble
had indeed extended to cole and daddy-o!

they've always had a sort of laurel & hardy back and forth
- though more gentle... no slap in the slap stick -
still a constant comedy routine flowing
with clever wit and wink o' the eye puns...
and saturday night they were in rare form... thus providing
an extra wonderful ride for me as their audience.

I sat down and held daddy-o's hand... he gripped it tighter
than usual... and did not let go during the playful romp
- he as captain with cole as his assistant –
on their "journey to the light"...
I was simply the young lady to his right and my presence
was needed for i "came from the light and knew how to
get back there... she has experience," daddy-o said...
When he asked me my name i said
"i don't know right now"... he liked this...
and when cole wanted to tell daddy-o my name he said..
"No! not knowing her name is part of the
mystery that will help us get to the light."...
so you know this made me fly even higher!

Now i don't know if daddy-o simply picked up
on my euphoric vibration from the ceremonial
celebration and coleman contact...
or if somehow energetically he received something
through the ethers... the love waves...
but I swear it was as if he had been there with us...
and he and i were buzzin' in an equal and
synchronistic montage of spiritual emotions...
it felt great and was really fun!!
and of course - hilariously funny with uncle cole sitting in
the side car... doing a splendid job as daddy-o's co-pilot!

finally by about 3:30 am it all simmered down
and eventually sleep came upon us.

today the journey isn't as fun for sweet daddy-o...
and by extension not as fun for me or
anyone on the daddy-o team...
he's having a hard time with little things...
the hiccups popping in every so often... like they are
sitting on the side-lines waiting for a vulnerable moment to
jump in and remind us all of what is really happening...
his soul is being pulled in one direction...
his body in another...
and there in the middle his tender diaphragm gets Yanked!

The struggle that accompanies this transition
has dimensions...
sometimes fun and entertaining… joyful even...
then in the blink of an eye the struggle can become
taxing and challenging...
most certainly harder to watch and allow.

And this is a whole rant for me... but in capsule form...
watching and allowing "the struggle" feels enormously
important!!... like that is where divine potential sits...
witnessing with acceptance and allowance…
is the clear cleansing rain...
giving... touching... feeding...
so the spiritual potential might bloom.

Whereas resisting the struggle...
judging it and squirming
in an effort to ward off and protect...
looking away or medicating it away...
well... this is what turns the struggle into suffering...

and since daddy-o is so in tune to everything right now...
including anyone near him...
if i turn his struggle into suffering
within my heart and energy...
then he is far more likely to take that on himself...
and suddenly his struggle turns into suffering as well...
soooo... more on that later ...

for now i send up a hallelujah! for our beloved coleman...
a hallelujah for sweet daddy-o!...
and a hallelujah for all of us...
as we await our band of angels...
comin' for to carry us home...
swing low sweet chariot... comin' for to carry us home...
goin' home!
lovelovelove

25... STRUGGLES

"oh me"... i'm feeling like the well is pretty darn dry...
but i'll try...
it's tuesday july 22nd and who would've imagined me still
being here in atlanta, georgia with my parents!... truly
remarkable and something i never could have predicted...
i mean if you told me i was going to be spending
more than a few weeks living with my parents
in their space - "not in this life time!"
And, of course, it isn't that my parents aren't wonderful
humans, it's just not natural for a child... or better to
say- not natural for this child!... I'm too independent and
adventurous. And I suppose it is actually an incredible
spiritual adventure in its own right. I read somewhere one
time "If you think you are a spiritually evolved adult, go
home and live with your parents... that's the true test."
and so i am... so it is...
And I must say it is also a test for said parents!!
(certainly with me it is anyway!;-)
And if i was grading i reckon i would give us all
B+'s... actually daddy-o would get an A+...
cause how could he get anything but!

And sometimes i think daddy-o is hanging on so we
- as a family - can get the potent lessons...
I said it to mama yesterday... this situation is a
golden window of opportunity for us to learn...
expand and grow...
and create more authentic relationships...
and daddy-o is holding space for us to do
such work... perhaps?? why not!
Yes - it all includes struggle... daddy-o's struggle
- the caterpillar busting out of the cocoon...

my struggle - revisiting all of my childhood born issues up close and personal! eeek!!... and mama's struggle...?
- i can only guess is watching those she loves dearly around her struggling and staying present without trying to fix things or squelch the struggles... I'm sure reid and rob and their families are having their own struggles too.

And when will the struggles end...?
Let's ask <u>Coleman</u>... I think - pretty pretty positive his struggle has ended...
and as i have been sitting with my own struggle... doing a sort of pingpong dance... some days able to rest in great gratitude for my current situation.... other days ready to run... i have been talking to coleman as if he is quite the expert... and he is saying... "Embrace the struggle! It is part of the precious gift of growth... which is why we choose to be human... to grow and learn and evolve! struggle equals learning... and when the struggle is wrapped in complete acceptance... well... there is no suffering."

Daddy-o is not suffering... he'll have days of being a bit more needy... or seeming a little depressed... but those days are a small scattering within a bounty of cheerful vibrancy... And the main amazement is his acceptance!
He is riding through this uncharted territory with acceptance... he is walking through the darkness with trust... and so he is able to laugh with me when i ask him how he is feeling this morning...?
and he answers... "well, okay... except for some reason i woke up on the floor laying inside this basket!"
"oh me!"
lovelovelove

From an article in The New Yorker, Feb 9, 2015 entitled
The Trip Treatment: Research into psychedelics, shut down for decades,
is now yielding exciting results.
By Michael Pollan.

Many researchers I spoke with described
their findings with excitement,
some using words like "mind-blowing." Bossis said,
"People don't realize how few tools we have in psychiatry
to address existential distress.
Xanax isn't the answer.
So how can we not explore this, if it can recalibrate how we die?"
(Anthony Bossis is a co-principal investigator for the N.Y.U. trial
with a specialty in palliative care.)

26... RESTING IN THE RIDDLE

saturday morning... july 26...
and the theme for the moment is poco a poco...
little by little...
perhaps the expression most shared by my
Peruvian friends... to me anyway.
Poco a poco they would say when i would feel shy
or embarrassed regarding how slowly my spanish
language skills were developing... or poco a poco as
i would give a wide-eyed expression regarding our
mountain top destination while hiking... or poco a poco
as i showed confusion and dismay as i blundered
some cultural custom at a community event...
poco a poco...

little by little...
and what spiritual virtue needs to be in
accompaniment for poco a poco to work...?
yep... the big P...
the ultimate challenge for those of us from this
caffeine soaked - accomplishment bound -
ambitious rat on endless track - style culture!! "oh my!"...
And so one of the greatest teachings from my
time thus far in peru is getting tested!!...
how Patient am I...???
have all those poco a poco's actually sunk in somewhat...
has the potent patience of an indigenous culture who has
weathered the constant trample of impatient conquerors
actually integrated into my spirit...?

Daddy-o's helping to give me a wonderful reflection...

The amazing peruvian patience is swaddled in
a divine trust... like they aren't in charge...
the mystery is...
and what is supposed to be accomplished
or what is supposed to come to light...
will... when it is supposed to...
and so they walk holding hands with the mystery...
with trust and patience.

Daddy-o has often spoken to me about this virtue...
he calls it "resting in the riddle"... i like that!
And he is helping all of us right now to
rest in the riddle with patience...
the riddle of his coming and going! "oh me!"...
changin' his mind and takin' his time...
poco a poco... it is up to the mystery...

And today i feel very patient...
say there isn't a better place to be... than resting in
the mystery... the riddle tickling me with delight...
and that is a good day...
and much of it has to do with the fact that daddy-o...
mama too... are chillin' and feeling good...
not a lot of struggle going on for the past week or so...
no hiccups.... no sleepless nights... no sad feelings...
visitors bringing good cheer...

in keeping that brings up another noticing...
how much easier it is to be patient... resting in the riddle...
when Struggle isn't very present...

Therefore the ultimate challenge is...
drum roll please...
hugging the struggle with arms of great patience...
isn't it?... and indeed…
that is what the indigenous peoples of the world have
done probably more than any other group of humans...
Hug the Struggle!
and that takes deep patience!
wrapped in deep trust!

And so i send up mountains of gratitude shouting...
Thank you <u>Roberto Canal Luna</u>!!! and the rest
of my peruvian helpers and teachers...
your sharings and lessons are carrying me now...
i am eternally grateful for the patience and acceptance
you all have shown me and so infused into me...
poco a poco...
my heart flutters with love and yearning
for the beautiful and magical beings
of my sweet peruvian world!

And Thank you Daddy-o!!!!...
as you walk your last chapter with deep patience
and deep trust...
giving me and those around you the opportunity as well...
the opportunity for us to rest in your riddle...
for us to patiently bear witness to your
mystical transformation...
as you also define beautiful and magical being!!...
not to mention teacher extraordinaire!
lovelovelove

A spirit molecule needs to elicit, with reasonable reliability,

certain psychological states we consider "spiritual".

These are feelings of extraordinary joy, timelessness,

and a certainty that what we are experiencing is more real than real.

Such a substance may lead us to an acceptance

of the coexistence of opposites,

such as life and death, good and evil;

a knowledge that consciousness continues after death;

a deep understanding of the basic unity of all phenomena;

and a sense of wisdom or love pervading all existence.

- DMT- The Spirit Molecule by Rick Strassman

27... WHAT YOU SEE IN DIFFERENT PIECES IT'S ALL IN ONE PIECE!

oh my goodness... it's already august... day
3 of month 8... half infinity of infinity...
can we have half infinity...? and what is infinity really...?
pure unity...?
Right now, i am thinking that unity is the answer
to just about everything!
Daddy-o said it night before last... in the wee morning
hours he blurted out - with impressive volume! -

"It's all in one piece!... It's all in one piece!...
It's all in one piece!...
What you see in different pieces... It's all in one piece!!!"

I was sleeping in the bed next to daddy-o for mama
was in the mountains - her first night away since he
took to his bed... since i had been snoozing he wasn't
necessarily talking to me as much as just allowing
a revelation to be released...
out into the world for whoever might grasp it...

And there it is... the grasping...
i do believe we are surrounded by mystical revelations...
All.The.Time!
and most often our grasp does the opposite
and sweeps them away...

83

I have emphasized in several posts that daddy-o has been
drug free... i had no intention for this to be a bragging...
but a telling...
that his mystical wanderings and revelations
have been just that...
many times i have heard folk talk about the final words
of their loved ones as drug induced hallucinations...
and certainly there might be some of that... and i also
feel after experiencing daddy-o's journey for this long...
that what our culture tells us to call hallucinations
might actually often be mystical revelations...

oh my! how the mystics have suffered through the ages...
burned or thrown into mental institutions...
why are we, as a culture, so afraid of the mystery...?
as well, the folk who are more in touch with it...?
especially our loved ones so close to the mystical
doorway... why do we medicate them so much...?

of course my vision is different after living
in peru for the past five years... where the
mystical is more a part of everyday life...

The indigenous cultures and their shamanic traditions
throughout the world - including peru - have encouraged
"death practices"...
certain rituals and ceremonies where
individuals or communities can practice slipping over
to the mystical world...
returning of course
to then live life with less fear
and more mystical understanding...

Our culture has always "outlawed" mystical journeying...
but guess what y'all!... daddy-o is doing it anyway!
breakin' the law breakin' the law... naturally, as is his style.
And oh what amazing teachings he is sharing...
for those who might grasp...
"what you see in different pieces... it's all in one piece."

Otherwise we are all rollin' along...
still doing some back and forth dancing...
the day after his "one piece" proclamation... daddy-o was
asking me to push him backwards... his bed is against the
wall so i told him that felt difficult... he looked so sad...
i asked him why he wanted me to push him backwards...
and he said "because everything that is important to me
is behind me"... Ouch!
the mystical potential no longer inviting...
the riddle no longer inspiring... in this moment...

though i am sure it will return... as it seems to be
built into the fabric of the whole experience...

i read recently that Steve Jobs (creator of apple
computers) had his final words voted as the most
important quote of the year... he looked over the
shoulders of his gathered loved ones and said
"Oh wow. oh wow. oh wow."

Final words... mystical revelations... wonders...
miracles... they are all here...
gifts awaiting our notice... gentle grasping...
open love palm... waiting with patience...
thank you daddy-o for all of it!
Lovelovelove

My view has evolved to seeing death – the

moment of death – as a ceremony.

If people are sitting with you help as you are going through

this dying ceremony,

help them to see you as the soul you truly are, not as your ego.

If they identify you as your ego,

during the last part of this ceremony, they will cling to you

and pull you back instead of facilitating your transformation.

-Ram Dass (ramdass.org)

28... GATRA'S WORDS

Friday August 8th mom's post.... I am a poor substitute for Winn in writing updates on Bill but she has been unable to get this done this week.....and there are changes. Bill has had the tough hiccups for a week now and in the last two days has begun "his journey".....being awake most of the time and talking most of this time. Some of his dialogue becomes conversation and some does not make much sense. He is comfortable as best we know...despite wanting to get out of that bed (in bed, unable to do anything for himself, since the first week of May). His patience and politeness have been amazing. Since Thursday afternoon, Bill has talked of panels that must be dealt with, some five and then two....and their leading to peace, love and hope. At one point, he said, "My friends, one opportunity to count the number of panels for our fellow citizens and memory of their pilgrimage to this place. For those who do not choose, the rest of us on this pilgrimage bid you a temporary or permanent farewell...... anyone that wishes, take a hand and pull gently backwards so the pilgrimage will be on the right track. Gently pull, gently pull and we will begin to move away from our board #1." Later he said, "on the side of hope, and peace and love, let us turn to the help we have at hand....for those who will grasp one another and help the community to move gently but definitely in the direction of peace and love and hope"........ and so the richness and struggle of these days continue...... as we pray for this journey to be completed before too long. Thank you for your care, concern and love....your prayers. Gatra

Will matter then be destroyed or not?

The Savior replied, "Every nature, every modeled form, every creature,

exists in and with each other.

They will dissolve again into their own proper root.

For the nature of matter is dissolved into what belongs to its nature.

Anyone with two ears able to hear should listen!"

- Gospel of Mary Magdalene
-from The Gospel of Mary of Magdala: Jesus and the First Woman Apostle
by Karen L. King

29... THE WINDOW THAT IS WISDOM'S WAYS

progression... the journey not the destination...
the web and how every little wind blows through all...
thy will not my will - and thank goddess hallelujah!!...
wee notions on my mind
this sunday early afternoon august 17th...
thank you daddy-o... mucho mucho! i am so grateful we
are still walking together on this remarkable trail of non-
sense and dreamy aliveness... i think i am getting it a bit
more now! sorry not to be the quickest of students...
and i am here with what feels like a new level of stealth
and a keen awareness... discipline... discipleship...
spiritual energy of the puma...
warrior priestess... let's go... i can do
this... we can do this! i am yours!

i had a great visit with carol the hospice nurse and mary
the hospice social worker over a week ago now... mary
has been working hospice for 24 years... remarkable!...
she shared very helpful experiences as we sat
and compared the exit to the entrance.

Babies get the hiccups alot... so does daddy-o. Babies need
to be spoon fed... so does daddy-o. Once toddlers begin
getting words they can often talk non-sense or beyond-
sense (messages that come from a place beyond the
senses)... so does daddy-o. Babies do not have very much
control over themselves and their environment... same
with daddy-o. Babies get very little privacy... babies do not
have control over their elimination... babies are completely
dependent and have to count on the loving kindness of
those around them... babies get their will declined... often.

many similarities... and some big differences...
as babies are coming in their job is to create, learn
and grow through connection...
whereas for someone in their death bed
it is their job to let go of those connections...
multitudes of connections to let go of... oh me!...

mary said that we will most likely find daddy-o starting
to pull or push away... as he needs more autonomy
and gets ready to separate...
those to whom he feels most attached might be the ones
he pushes away the hardest or with more force...
he said to me one night after i had been rubbing his head,
"not too close, winndy"...
he has started dismissing us regularly from sitting at his
bedside... telling visitors he "needs to hibernate now" and
for them to please make themselves at home... to "please
take their patience and kindness and leave the room"...
sometimes even asking his beloved gatra to please leave...
always saying please and thank you as it is such
a part of his gentile southern gentry self.

another difference... babies come in with the task to
gain more control over themselves and their world...
the opposite is our task as we are exiting...
we must let go of control... whoa!
and we are talking immense levels of control...

mary and carol and i mused at how we celebrate a child
as potty training is attained!
Most parents remember the age she was and how it
happened... bragging rights... bronze the potty...;-)

and to the contrary on the other side
losing that control! oh dear!
it is at best ignored and swept away...
a horrifying thought to brag about it!
but let's think about it... really it is an incredible step
in the walk we call being human on planet earth...
an amazing feat of acceptance and humility... letting go!
since we are a culture founded in control it seems kooky
to celebrate losing control...
and perhaps this in itself is why it might be a good idea…
un-control celebration!

Mary also said that just as every woman and newborn
have their unique way of labor and entrance...
so does each human have their own unique way
of leaving this realm…
sometimes quick and easy.... sometimes slow and easy...
sometimes intense labor, sometimes not...
who knows the whys and wherefores...
part of the mystery.

Also "false labors" happen at both doorways...
daddy-o certainly has been a fan
of the false or practice labors...
and i am so grateful for each time he has "returned"
with a subtle shift allowing for those of us watching
to learn more of the process and open more
to the window that is wisdom's ways...
go daddy-o go!
lovelovelove

The strength to die

is a different kind of strength than we normally call upon.

It requires courage to go into the dark unknown.

But what is so wonderful about the first step is that,

once it is taken, the dark becomes light.

-*Sacred Dying: Creating Rituals for Embracing the End of Life*
by Megory Anderson

30... BALSAC OF THE WOODS

well dear friends, things have been quite different
today, this wednesday, august 20th...
daddy-o seems to be slippin' away for real this time!

today he has not responded to most inquiries... this
new silence has been a progression of fewer and fewer
words starting this past weekend... even questions of
sustenance "what kind of soup do you want...?" are
receiving blank stares.... when a soup is chosen for
him he will eat a little bit... but no more thank you's...
(which for all of you who know daddy-o well - very odd
not to hear gratitude for every little detail, isn't it)...
his breathing also has changed...
it reminds me of how i breath when i feel nauseous...
heavy steady trod-ding
to keep the feeling down down down...

we did have a little mini conversation yesterday
afternoon... he was looking disturbed or uneasy...
another new small twist in him of the last few days...
to give him something amusing i went to tell him that i just
received a phone call from a new friend named Sloth
while i was talking to a friend named Turtle...
can you say "hippie chick"... and proud of it!

anyway... i told him half the scenario and asked
if he could guess the name of the friend who
called in while i was talking to turtle...

93

he said "Balsac!"
I repeated it with a question mark and he then said
"Balsac of the woods"...
he said it with a tone of doom…
so i asked him if Balsac was dangerous?
he said "Yes!"

We sat in silence for a bit and one of his hands started
shaking under the cover so i placed my hand gently
on top of his shaking hand and he blurted out
"Be careful!" motioning with his eyes towards my
hand resting on top of his own, "In the woods!"
I quickly removed my hand.

After another pause Gatra returned and told us
she saw Edison (grandson) in his karate class...
"Edison got a signal!" he said with the doom tone...
as i stared with my eye brows lifted...
he added "Off to the woods"...
after another pause his hand started shaking again
and he got a pained look on his face...
i asked if he was hurting... he responded
"No, but you gotta hurt a little bit"... slight pause,
"in the woods."

So i guess sweet daddy-o was moving through
the frightening aspects of being in the woods.

Today he seemed peaceful... i did not witness
any disturbed or anxious expression...
he would meet my gaze when i would look up from what
i was reading... sometimes saying "hey" back to my "hi"...
sometimes just meeting my eyes in silence...
I played him some sweet spiritual music from Angela
Blueskies... it seemed to soothe him... it certainly did me.

It is hard to imagine that we might actually for real
be close to the final transition!
I just kind of got my 2nd... or 3rd... or 4th! wind...
ready and feeling charged to keep sailing on
with him however long he desired...
changing my future agenda all around once more...
and feeling good about it...
and excited to have more time with him...
to hear more of his wonderful beyond-sensical musings...
to rub his head as long as he'll let me...
to soak up every little drop
of his sweetness and goodness that i possibly can...

and now it seems i might only hear a few more
precious words... daddy-o's magical words...
he is a master of language...
and now he is silent...
and even though i have been preparing for this
for many moons now...
i don't like it!
his silence sucks!
it's breaking my heart to pieces...
with tears of lovelovelove

31... A LITTLE SHOW TO DO

and so beautiful friends... daddy-o is back to talking!!
this friday morning august 22nd after responding
to my 'hi" with his usual "hey"
he said "you and i have a little show to do."
well okay daddy-o! let's go do the show...
what's that old expression... the show must go on...
and so it is.

yesterday he started the day talking to
gatra about "crossing over"...
he said "this morning I will cross over"...
and after a long pause he said
"you understand I don't fully know what all this means."
Then a little later when i was with him and asked if
there was anything i could do for him he said
"how am i gonna transfer and get up yonder...
got any clues?"
oh sweet daddy-o... so precious.

and the clues i have...
well they can't be expressed or understood with
any verbal language or in an intellectual way...
and so i have been trying energetically to mimic
the "struggle" and the "letting go"...
without really realizing...
just allowing myself to be guided...
but now i can see a little bit... maybe...
the window clear one moment and murky the next...

after Coleman's transition i thought a lot about
"struggle"… it had already been a current theme
watching daddy-o in his moments of struggle...
i think i wrote something in a past post...
how resisting the struggle is when it turns into suffering...
whereas being present to it with acceptance
keeps it at the level of struggle…
which isn't necessarily hard or negative...
it just is.

so sitting with coleman and daddy-o...
holding their struggles in my heart...
i started looking and opening to my struggles...
especially the main one i could remember coating my
childhood... eight years old after school "numb-out"...
i slip into the pantry...
secretly i mix butter and powdered sugar... stir it up...
inject it down... ooh wee sugar and fat...
feel the buzz release the angst...
not really too different from coleman's needle
and spoon struggle scenario...
except my drug is legal and encouraged...
and probably actually destroys more lives than heroin...
it certainly has made me want to say from time to time...
"i'm done i'm spent kaput i quit!

so my life long struggle...
sugar and fat and the buzzbuzzbuzz...

okay coleman okay daddy-o... help me figur' how to
accept my struggle with love and compassion
and then perhaps... whoa! could it be...
that might lead to letting go...!? letting go of what..?

well firstly that nasty ol' suffering!
accept the struggle as an incredible god-given challenge
to help me in my soul's work...?
hoe-kay! that's extreme...
deep breath!

so i signed up (with gatra's full encouragement
and support for which i am super grateful!!)
to do a three week nutritional cleanse
with my friend, Ellen Kittredge...

so for the past almost three weeks i have been
letting go of very old notions...
old shields that probably helped protect me as a
wee one but for many years now have just been
weighing me down - literally and figuratively!!

the cleanse has been intense!... and awesome!!

so accepting the struggle and letting go...
can you feel it daddy-o...?
i'm with you... let's do this show!!!
lovelovelove

Wake up lovers, it is time to start the journey!

We have seen enough of this world, it is time to see another.

These two gardens may be beautiful but let us pass beyond them

and go to the Gardener.

Let us kiss the ground and flow like a river towards the ocean.

- Rumi

Translation by Coleman Barks

32... NEW MOON AND NEW MISSIONS

Daddy-o report following your friendly astrological news...

And i quote June Collier.... www.astrologywithjune.com...
New Moon in Virgo August 25, 2014...
"Yikes! Whoa Nellie! Holy shit! Mars is conjunct Saturn in
Scorpio! Have we got a full head of steam going yet?
Do we know where the relief valve is? Can you feel, see,
hear, smell and taste the brassy buzz of insanity?
Are we suffocating in a self-destructive soup of separation,
selfishly seeking safety through power, control and
authority? Shiva gives life and she takes it away.
Death is the transformation of one form of
consciousness into another. Death is the end
of illusions, and a spiritual re-birthing.
Conjunctions are when two or more planets are within
at least 10 degrees of each other. This brings an
intensification of the energies of the planets involved and
an expression of that energy in a focused way at the sign
and degree of the perfection of the conjunction. New
Moons are always the conjunction of the Moon and Sun
each month and bring new beginnings and an emphasis
of the energy of the sign and degree. The New Moon
on August 25, 2014 is perfect at 10:13 am EDT....."
(to read the rest visit June's site!)

At 10:13-ish this morning daddy-o, reid, mama
and myself were having a wonderful conversation
about starting a "new mission"...
I walked into the room, gatra was already there,
and daddy-o said...
"Hi! I expect to see you on down the road here...
Can I catch a ride...?"

I responded something like - sure okay and are we gonna just see where that road takes us..? Daddy-o said, "And maybe more that we see HOW it gets us there." Ah-ha!

Reid entered the room... and after greetings and howyadoins'... daddy-o said "This is a whirlygig in a difficult series... in the ceiling fan a difficult series... and we have a problem where this fan goes to..."

Now to give a little history - the whirlygig or ceiling fan has been a point of conversation many times... almost a character of its own in the daddy-o show or story... Usually its name is whirlygig... and it is some sort of symbol within the beyond-sensical mystical language daddy-o has been using. And obviously it is also some sort of portal.

After we asked questions about what was the "difficult series" with little response... daddy-o said "Now reid, are you presumably on some mission or course...?" Reid said my mission right now is to be with you... this comment led into a long conversation about daddy-o's new mission... how right now it is the mission of all of us (the daddy-o team) to be accompanying him as he leaves one mission to start a new... Reid said something about we see you getting ready to leave one mission - the mission of raising us kids and being a husband and teaching thousands of students – now you've completed that mission and it is time to start a new mission... perhaps.

Reid also said "And it is okay with us for you to start that new mission whenever you are ready to do it." Daddy-o said "Ah, well."

daddy-o asked me if i had a mission and i said that right
now it was to learn from him... witnessing how he was
changing his mission... sailing in uncharted territory...
he is the captain and i am part of his crew...

after more back and forth regarding missions...
gatra asked "are you comfy with your new mission..?"
he said, "No! ordinarily i'm supposed to come to the
end of this rope or roadway and reach some kind of
happy resolution!"... oh me!
so then we all talked about how just because his
mission was changing didn't mean we would not all
still be together... he and gatra have had a wonderful
theme going on saying how they will always be
connected in the same love...
reid re-iterated it saying connected in spirit and love.
I suggested that he may actually be closer to all
that he loves once in his new mission...
and we said we will always be with you sweet daddy-o...
wherever your new mission takes you...

and so we are... circled up in the darkness
of new moon and new missions...
it's scary to walk in the dark... to face our
new missions... why do we do it...?
because we have to! it's our job...
to know birth and death and re-birth...
i suppose it's the main mission for us wee humans on
planet earth... definitely inescapable... just gotta do it...
nerve-rackin' knee-knockin' hold-your-nose-and-jump
kinda thang on the everlasting to do list!
go daddy go! you are soooo held!
lovelovelove

Flee from being scattered and being in bondage,

and then you already have resurrection.

If you know what in yourself will die, though

you have lived many years,

why not look at yourself and see yourself risen now?

You have the resurrection, yet you go on as if you are to die

when it is only the part destined to die that is moribund.

-The Treatise on Resurrection

The Gnostic Bible, Edited by Willis Barnstone and Marvin Meyer

33... SIGNALS AND A GIFT
ALREADY GIVEN

Friday, august 29th... good labor
celebration to you all dear friends!
an interesting concept the celebration of labor...
and i would say that daddy-o has been feeling
the labor of his situation and present perspective…

for the past three days or so he has
been doing lots of gazing...
lifting his head slightly and gazing down past his feet...
or scanning the space between him and the ceiling...
landing for moments at a time in certain spots
and just gazing...
he also has been eye gazing...
he and i have just been gazing into each other's eyes
for long stretches!...
without any words... just intense connection via our eyes...
at first it was hard for me... super intense!
just Really! hard to do…
and then there are the judgments…
is this okay... is this proper?...
but then I find the strength
and cast judgment to the wind…
and so have been beaming as much love and adoration
as i can conjure into his sweet eyes...
and we have done this for long! stretches...
i'm talking 30 mins between little snippets of words...
did I already say ?– it's intense!!

in between his gazing daddy-o's expressions have been
mixed... wednesday morning he woke up and said to gatra
"I can't believe i am in this morning!...
is this real? is this real?"
later in the day i asked him if he was feeling good
and peaceful... he said "i think so... i keep waiting
for signals of where i am supposed to be."
we talked for a while about these signals and what
they might look or feel like... no clear ideas came out
though except that they had something to do with
"doorways or entrances"...
I asked if there was anything we could do
to encourage the signals and he responded
"No i don't... i think we have to wait our best
opportunities and see what develops."
he asked me "you haven't had any signals come your
way?" i said i wasn't sure... then he said "have you had
any signals of being... partial signals instead of fully
social?" again not sure... "well that's a fair answer."

I have to admit that part of the eye gazing on my
account has to do with not having what feels like the
right words to say... i need a mystical language... i want
to chant or drum or smudge... not daddy-o's style...
prayer! hey daddy-o wanna pray? and he did...
lovely beautiful prayer
"Precious god... we thank you for encouraging us to ask
to be open to your guidance... so that we might know your
will for your people.... in jesus name we pray... amen."

okay that took up two minutes… back to eye gazing...
i suppose this is the mystical language we need right now.

At one point I asked daddy-o what was his favorite bible story... he said "the story of adam and eve".... i asked why?... "well it's the one that jumps up at you."

Later that evening he said to gatra... "be sure everyone knows what light they are under and why"...

I don't think he slept that night or not until the wee hours... just gazing... looking around in the spaces... waiting for signals...?
In the morning... again upon waking he expressed distress to gatra that he was still here!
Later in the afternoon he said it to uncle cole... "i don't understand why i am still here?"
And we don't know really if he is talking about leaving this realm or if he is frustrated that he is confined to bed and is wanting to get better and get up... where is he really..? what's really going on in his heart...? why is he still here..? why is he in bed...?
it's all a mystery really... and gazing seems the essence...

Then he surprised me last night and exclaimed "winndy! do you have a sense of how simple it is..?" then he said "amazing and simple... amazing and so simple!"
i asked how is it so amazing and so simple..?
"A gift!"... then a long pause...
"A gift to my heart"... then another long pause....
"This is a gift yet it is already given."

and so we are... sitting in the gift... as it is already given... with gratitude and lovelovelove

Light and Darkness, life and death, right and left,

are brothers of one another.

They are inseparable.

Because of this neither are the good good, nor evil evil,

nor is life life, nor death death.

For this reason each one will dissolve into its earliest origin.

But those who are exalted above the world are indissoluble, eternal.

-Gospel of Philip, logion 9, Translation by Wesley W. Isenburg

34... COLEMANIA'S CHARGE

oooh wee! still reelin' y'all... tuesday sept 2...
the love and energy of <u>Coleman</u>'s musical celebration
still chargin' my cellular self...
what an honor!
we celebrated his authenticity and sensitivity and verve
with just that...
a musical extravaganza where everyone stole
the show cause there was no show...
it was real and intimate and beyond ourselves...
sacred ceremony in the guise of *Colemania!*...
circle of broken hearted love snuggles
with magical music holding us... rockin us...
helping us ascend out of our grief armor
and into mushy mystical connection...
feeling individual human while at the same time tribal spirits
creating wholeness and holiness... whoa! extraordinary!

super dooper kudos to all of us!!!
and special shout out to my brother <u>Rob </u>for the weaver
he is... keepin the lines flowin and hearts open!
as well as to the high priestess of the ceremony... my soul
sista <u>Claire</u>... with her divine wisdom and bulging bag of
magic tricks she sculpted a mighty chalice that hugged
us all with ease and freedom and a charge of truth!...
such a container is a rare and special gift.

And of course... there was our sweet coleminer...
so present!
stirring it up with his relaxed charm
and sincere enthusiasm...
holding each individual - special personal tender...
while at the same time holding all of us...
and in his holding still sharing
perhaps one of his most potent love abilities...
for the little for the big for the one for the many...
he gave... and still gives... acceptance...
pure sweet simple acceptance...
with a wink and a poke and a pirate joke... acceptance...
one of the highest so called virtues we wee humans might
attain... he never turned his back... modeling for us...

and at the same time giving his close beloveds
a great challenge to do the same for him...
an interesting paradox...

i've been thinking during this death march of a summer...
how perhaps the highest honor we might give
our beloveds who cross before us
is to acknowledge their most potent virtue/s
and ask them for an infusion...
a dose...
a download...

oh sweet coleminer... help me to be more
accepting... judgment is a heavy burden to bear
and i am tired.

on the daddy-o side of the tracks...
he was lively and "out there" last night...
talking about the backdoor as opposed to the frontdoor...
where the signals are guiding us...
i don't have my notes with me so more details later...

earlier in the afternoon we had a special treat as the
guys from *Red Rainbow* (our *Colemania!* band) came
over and we played for daddy-o... surrounding him in
an acoustic sound of our set from the night before...
Leavey playin percussion on the old chesto'drawers
from dad's grandmother... rob and paul piled on mama's
bed next to his... foster strummin at his feet... and
me sittin by his side... with edison (rob's boy) playin
rhythm by throwin a rubber ball against the wall...
it was a brilliant love nest swaddling daddy-o
in our residual spiritual high...
he LOVED it!
and sang along... cheering us on as always...
supa supa precious scene!!

so we close the dog days of summer...
this potent deep swelter of a summer...
with an explosion of bittersweet liquid light
flowing through notes of musical ritual...
still holding a waiting trust with daddy-o...
grief armor needed longer but lighter as fall approaches...
feeling coleman's loving hand of acceptance...
waiting open and receiving
should daddy-o need a wee pull...
holding them close and releasing them to be free...
always...
lovelovelove!

On Jordan's stormy banks I stand,
And cast a wishful eye
To Canaan's fair and happy land,
Where my possessions lie.

Refrain
I am bound for the promised land,
I am bound for the promised land
Oh who will come and go with me?
I am bound for the promised land.

O the transporting, rapturous scene,
That rises to my sight!
Sweet fields arrayed in living green,
And rivers of delight!
Refrain
There generous fruits that never fail,
On trees immortal grow;
There rocks and hills, and
brooks and vales,
With milk and honey flow.
Refrain
O'er all those wide extended plains
Shines one eternal day;

There God the Son forever reigns,
And scatters night away.
Refrain
No chilling winds or
poisonous breath
Can reach that healthful shore;
Sickness and sorrow,
pain and death,
Are felt and feared no more.
Refrain
When I shall reach
that happy place,
I'll be forever blest,
For I shall see my Father's face,
And in His bosom rest.
Refrain
Filled with delight my raptured soul
Would here no longer stay;
Though Jordan's waves around me
roll, Fearless I'd launch away.

-- in a minor mode,
traditional hymn by Samuel
Stennett (1727-1795)

112

35... SPIRITUAL GEL

post #2 for this tuesday sept 2...
in between another bout of hiccups...
sweet daddy-o said to mama this morning...

"I need some spiritual gel!"

oh my goodness!...
so putting out the call to all of you...
our friends and family and wonderful
community of beloveds...
please send sweet daddy-o some spiritual gel...
whatever that looks and feels like to you...
let's lube him up!
with the sweetest smellin'... yummiest feelin'...
slip slidin'est spiritual gel we can imagine and conjure!!!

with gratitude and
lovelovelove!

36... LEAN BACK IN A GLOBAL CHAIR

i am still marinating y'all... this thursday sept 4th...
in the loving kindness of facebook birthday greetings...
gracias a todo!!
especially nice because i chose to stick close to
daddy-o yesterday... woke up with no plans and was
greeted with lovely notes posted around the house by
mama whispering sweet reflections into mine eyes...
then enjoyed the morning with her and daddy-o...
mama pulling up memories from my childhood
in between daddy-o's wild romp...
he's been in yet another - what i call - "labor phase"...
since monday i suppose...

monday night we had a time where he was having
"some unexpected friends...
well we stopped by to get some water so that is nice."
he'll say these things while glancing into the space
in the room between himself and the ceiling...
just sweeping and staring at points...
"that whole business of coming in the back way in
order to gain attention from a different direction"...
he was slightly agitated and went on and on
about the back door...
"in fact this back doorway...
not to encourage... people to use the back doorway"...
"problem... i mean there's so much hoot
and holler about the back door"...

the back door conversation went on for a
good bit with long pauses throughout...
"have we had any more signals about the back door?...
knocks or clarifications...
well we've got our right hand plank... and here's
our back door if it has any interest in being...
i think it doesn't have any interest in
being part of our front door..."

And the manner of the conversation was that of one of
his seminar groups... him leading a group of students
or colleagues in critical theological wanders
or ethical problem solving –
"but i think we've done quite well with coming on"...
"now folks consider that"... and the like...

When i told him i was gonna go make myself a cup
o' tea he said... "i think that is a good idea because
time and interest and space are working on us..."

We ended that romp with
"i'm beginning to get a sense of coming apartness
which isn't very nice."
His hands started fumbling under the covers
so i pulled them back...
"just pull it off!" he said meaning the covers
"we don't have to abide by their regulations!"

After a pause with the covers down
i asked if he was still coming apart...?
"No, i don't feel like i am coming apart... to
the contrary i'm being restored."

In the wee morning hours the hiccups began
again and have been consistent since.

Yesterday morning's romp started with daddy-o saying...
"i want to lean back in a global chair"...

later he was directing gatra and me...
"dear, could you and winn move in such a way
to bring these two sides into light"...
we stood at either end of his bed...
"ok, let's see now... help me get across this big leap."

This morning he said...
"not like this earth... more like another earth"...
"sorta begin to turn toward this earth and away from the
other one." After a long pause... "every now and then i get
a feeling of poetry... that could be like a poem... yeah"...
after another long pause... "the skies are so bright."

Carol the hospice nurse came today... and she
said her sense was this might not be another
"practice labor"
but that perhaps he really is close...
certainly his jargon is all about it, isn't it...
"i want to lean back in a global chair"!!!...
ooh wee! me too, daddy-o!...
and his comment from the last post...
"I need some more spiritual gel"...

He's moving... he's working... he's laboring...
re-birthing himself into his global chair...

the re-birth canal is a tricky place it seems...
always there... always so close!...
at the same time preciously elusive...
tentative... and oh so thin...
a transparency of membrane between
will and allowance...
focused concentration and dreamy openness...
control and letting go...

so keep sending that spiritual gel y'all!!...
envision him sliding through that birthdeath canal
lubed up with ease and grace and divine order...
send cheers of encouragement and wonder...
celebration of the miracle!

resurrection stories aren't in every spiritual
or religious tradition just cause...
they tell the divine truth...
resurrection is real...
let's send up a hoop and a holler as daddy-o
says... whether it's the backdoor or not...
holler yeeeeedawgie! go daddy-o go!!!!!
you're so close baby...
your minions are cheering you on!! we celebrate you!
we celebrate your journey!
we celebrate your transition!
we celebrate your resurrection!...

celebratin' and squirtin' the finest spiritual gel you can
imagine!!... cause you are so fine... sweet daddy-o!

and if not... that's okay too...
lovelovelove

[Andean] legend and lore tell us that after death

the physical body goes back to the earth,

our knowledge returns to the mountains,

and our essence or soul returns to the stars.

The shaman has given us a map for this journey beyond death,

describing three stages or opportunities

for us to recognize our luminous nature.

-Alberto Villoldo via *dyingconsciously.com*

37... LET IT BE

hola amorcitos.... ooh wee... a nice cool
fall feeling day in atlanta ga! okay!!
today, sept 15th, used to be marked as the day i would
be boarding my return flight to peru... and how wonderful
of the divine to give me an opportunity to relax into
un-scheduling and letting it be...
and god said, "Let it be"... and with that poof! out plopped
the universe... that's some power, eh? i reckon creative
energy must like those three little words... let it be...
and so i will and so i am.

in the teachings i have learned within my peruvian world
the quechua word "ayni" contains the same teaching...
let it be equals
let it go equals do not cling equals always share...
in fact always share with reckless generosity
equals empty oneself equals true connection...
true connection to the divine creative energy
we sometimes call god...

ooh wee that fall air has got me shouting it
from the mountain top!... let's party y'all!!!
throw all your gifts into the barrel and let's roll it down
the hill... through the valley and into the river... eventually
sinking into the depths of deep mystery... "Love
comes on strong, consuming herself, unabashed!"...
says Rumi "...having died to self-interest, she risks
everything and asks for nothing. Love gambles away
every gift God bestows!" Haku! Vamos! Let's go!

i am also fresh off of a silent retreat week where i read
wonderful books and wrote and sat in my dreams
meditating and visioning... allowing myself to indulge in
the want of a contemplative mystic... ahhhh... so good!!
also re-membering... the old winn that was…
before may 5th when daddy-o decided to lie down...
before may 31st when Coleman decided to sail away...
before august 31st when *Colemania!* gave stage
to a priestess of grief and gratitude...
the heart break so miraculously horrible and wonderful
that sacred sensations and wisdoms found room...
gurgling up through the cracks...
exposure... vulnerability... authenticity!!
engulfed in flame yet cold to the touch...
who am i now...?
who am i when coleman visits in my dreams, wrapping
me in divine love bliss beyond description...? who am i
when daddy-o and i eye gaze for eternal moments...?
who am i as a yearning... a wailing desperate yearning...
to be free... to be connected... to be Love...
to gamble away every gift God bestows…
so i might truly know... truly feel... truly give...
and thus truly receive!
oh me!... see what that contemplative mystic stuff does to
me... anyone wanna go dancing..? .... i need to shake!

So daddy-o's most recent "labor phase" even
fooled the hospice nurse... He's back!!
which helped facilitate my retreat... often after those
laborious days he returns to a place of being where
i feel less needed... him more needing the solidity of
gatra and their energetic threads... less desirous of the
grim reaper with red hair and a winn wink... no really!

i shift and so welcome his state of being as best i can
discern it... and when he is talking about "the ending" and
"going home"... i open myself with enthusiastic willingness
to do my damnedest... to journey as far as i can with him...
shielding away the fears and judgments...

and i feel like such the novice!... fumbling along
in a game that is way over my head really...
still yet, charged by faint melodies tickling my heart...
ancestral rocking pushing me along... trust in the mystery,
trust in the mystery, she sings... great goddess of death
and re-birth... trust in the mystery… and so i try... so i do.

after spending days in the outside world returning
to his side once more... i feel as if i have re-
entered through some sheer curtains
back into a sacred space slightly askew...
a dimension subtly off or surreal...
where lying in bed equals really hard work...
words have different meanings... looking down at the
end of the bed or staring out into space represent
wonders far beyond current comprehension...
and where thinking about the future really is useless...
predicting outrageous...
so just being... complete and absolute being...
is the wavy wave to catch and ride...
in this temple of acceptance...
enjoying and marveling in each precious moment...
knowing on down the road once this sacred surreal
space has disappeared... i will have days when
i desire to dredge it back as best i can...
missing it... missing him...
lovelovelove

Those who say the Lord died first and (then) rose up are in error,

for he rose up first and (then) died

If one does not first attain the resurrection,

he will not die.

-*Gospel of Philip, logion 22, Translation by Wesley W. Isenburg*

38... HEART SONG FOR MAMA

Mmmmmm feeling a heart song for mama today...
a sweet melody to compliment this bright fresh
fall splendor of a magical sunday...
september 28th... a precious moment... as they all are...

I have been up here in these sweet grandmother mountains
surrounding asheville, nc for the past 5 nights...
bringing all the heavy material accouterments that give
definition to this life of mine down from the attic...
bustin' through the bags and boxes... sorting through...
letting go... holding on... letting go.... holding on...
"but i might need this if".... "well, one day if this is my
future i need it.... but if that is my future i don't"...
bouncing like a crazy neon colored bouncy ball
between decisions... every so often collapsing onto the
sofa and resting in a hut-on-the-beach-fantasy...
rising up to answer the phone for the next estimate on
a new roof... "ah! $600 cheaper and a sexy man
who speaks spanish...
we'll go with that one!"...

walking through the charming neighborhood that holds
us -me and the adorable little log cabin some paper tells
me is mine... reuniting with friends and neighbors...
opening to their reflections and warmth with new eyes
and spirit as the past 5 years i've been gone...
gonegonegone...
living in a story far outside my comfort zone...
with immense gratitude…
the learning and growth equal to the stretch...

And i must say to have this wee respite
back in a super snuggle comfy smoochie love zone!...
well, it's a throw up my arms into the air
and sing hallelujah!! kind of welcomed treat!
thank you asheville!!!!

And thank you mama!!! So in the meantime
Gatra is holding down the daddy-o front solo...
my brothers are close and very supportive and their lives
are very full! So really she's basically on her own...
doing a bouncy dance as well... letting go... holding on...
letting go... holding on... as sweet daddy-o continues in
his wavy walk... one conversation focused on the bridge
he must cross or the door that needs to be open...
and the next interlude back as his professor-self needing
to prepare for the coming seminar or teaching event...
as I've mentioned he said to me back in march
"I feel my role as bill mallard is complete but I've had so
much fun I don't want to give it up."... and so it is...
he has fully embraced this life and his path and his roles...
dressing it all in fun fun fun!
It's really hard to leave a good party.
I have had many a sleepless nights
myself for the very same reason.

We celebrate his wavy walk...
as his mid-wives we are committed to giving him
as wonderful a crossing as we possibly can...
And it isn't easy.
But i just gotta tell y'all... that the Gatra Mallard who
has been showing up is offering me a vision of great
inspiration... Her loyalty and endurance and courage have
been off the charts!! She is always right by his side!

No breaks! And she has been riding his waves with a kind
of patience and flexibility I didn't know she had in her...
she is rising to the task...
she is growing through it all as well... her 79 year old self...
opening to the lessons...
receiving as best she can the messages...
messages from the mystery
that demand a different level of vulnerability...
heart-break cracking open her old beliefs and ideas...
So strong!!
Gatra is a special strength right now and she is
teaching me as much as sweet daddy-o and as much
as this miraculous journey we are on together....
so thanks mama!! para todo... you're a supa star!!!!

And, of course, as always... the other strength making
this journey possible is you all... beloved community!...
the love and prayers and spiritual gel you've been
sending is a gigantic Why we are able to do as well
as we are doing on the front line... knowing that we
have divine hugs backin' us is a gift beyond words!!

still i want more words in our language for gratitude...
there are so many levels...
and right now thinking of mama and daddy-o…
our family... this experience…
the community connection...
i don't have a word that feels big enough...
a word that feels as big as my heart swell.

so i'll fall back on the good ol' standard...
lovelovelove!

When you lose a loved one, you suffer.

But if you know how to look deeply, you have a chance to realize

that his or her nature is truly the nature of

no birth, no death.

There is manifestation and there is the cessation of manifestation

in order to have another manifestation.

You have to be very keen and very alert in order to recognize

the new manifestation of just one person.

But with practice and effort you can do it.

-No Death, No Fear by Thich Nhat Hanh

39... GETTING THE CALL AND ALLOWING THE FALL

October 21st...Hooooray for fall! de colores!...
swimming in golden hues the winds speak of letting go...
each little leaf allows itself to change...
to mature into a brilliant explosion of color...
and then it is asked to let go... just then!!??...
of all times to have to let go and fall away!?...
right as he is golden splendor...
right as he can look at his beautiful mature colors...
surrounded by vivid reflection...
a life well lived shown off in the breeze
waving like a wee flag of deep majestic brilliance!
and now he gets a call and has to let go and fall...
directionless carried on the whimsy of air... crumpling as
he goes... down to the ground... down to the humus...
richness crinkling into humility...
to be walked upon… raked up... or worst of
all blown by a harsh sounding machine... into
bunches with all the other fallen crowns.

The lucky ones are left alone… falling in the unkempt...
nourishing the soil that feeds their mother...
held in the cycle...
known eternally within the miracle of perfect design...
embraced as good helpful litter
blanketing the forest floor...
their letting go leading them to the next stage of their
contribution - gourmet nourishment for all of life...
top soil top shelf!...
a supa-charged cocktail of break down compost
wonder food… a crucial ingredient to this here movie
we call life on planet earth... thank you sweet leaf!

127

thank you for letting go... scary as it might be... that letting go leads you to a very important job... important for all... the All. And it is so with every being... is it not!?...

Perhaps our compulsive sweeping away of leaf litter can represent an interesting view into our confusion around "death"... Most of us don't notice or give awareness to the leaf's next job... therefore we also don't give kudos to its importance... acknowledging the cycle... the sweet leaf's "death" is actually just the start to its next job... its next vital contribution. And so it is with sweet daddy-o... and all of us.

One can give a physical diagnosis that bill mallard experienced a pulmonary embolism 2+ years ago and when the blood clot went through his heart it stopped, thus damaging the left side of his brain which is now slowly degenerating. Or one can give a spiritual diagnosis that bill mallard received a call - a call that his service was needed in his next phase... his next job awaiting... and scary as it might be for him and all of us who love him so... he must let go... we must let go... his golden colors are fading and his connection to the branch getting weaker... he has important work to do and this old body of his will soon no longer facilitate his work.

In the meantime I am eating up the teachings he is still able to give me and the beloveds who are close in... perhaps even folk far away... who knows... I just know that my life is being altered by the extension of his transition and i totally trust that it is for the best...

and it <u>is</u> hard!
I have been feeling like i need to be three in one recently...
Renovating my house in asheville... Bouncing back to
atlanta so gatra can actually take a much needed break –
Yeah mama!!! in the mountain house for three nights!!...
and receiving urgent calls from beloveds in peru
as my presence is needed there too...
all of it making me even more committed to learning how
to teleport sooner rather than later... anybody with me!?
my witchy-poo tingles tell me teleportation
is all about letting go as well...
and since the leaves are doing it right now it might
be the perfect time for all of us to practice...
how can you practice letting go?...
accompanying the leaves and sweet daddy-o...
and perhaps me too – if my teleportation scheme works...
i'll letyaknow !!

And so uncle cole and i are holding down home
base until mama gets back tomorrow...
then on friday the professor bill mallard will be celebrated
as one who contributed vital ingredients to the history
of his beloved candler school of theology...
golden splendor!
surrounded by vivid reflection of a life well lived...

just in time to let go and float beyond such pageantry...
no time to rest on his laurels... he has received the call...
and in divine right timing he will heed the call...
on to his next vital contribution...
maybe it'll be helping us all learn to teleport!
now wouldn't that be golden.
lovelovelove

40... EL DIA DE LOS MUERTOS

Nov 1st.... My favorite celebration I've yet experienced
in the peruvian village of ollantaytambo
el dia de los muertos - the day of the dead...
which follows today's fiesta
el dia de los vivos – the day of the living...
ahhh harmony.

For day of the dead we gathered in the village
cementario taking time to spruce up the graves...
a little paint... some flowers... different decorations...
gathering the stones to place back on top of the mound...
caring details.
As the village family gathered throughout the day
more and more refreshments came...
picnic style sit on top of grandma and enjoy
some rico delicioso morsels and cerveza...
always giving some to grandma as well...
little music combos showing up eventually adding sweet
and simple tunes to the festive acknowledgment of the
ancestors... stories and gratitude flowing in stream with
the cerveza... laughter and tears wrapping around the
hardships and the joys as the past is recounted...
dancing praying sharing communing...
vital community...
re-membering to-gether...
the ancestors oh so present...
time as a spiral or a weaving... allowing room
for creative connection and important reflection...
"someday they will be toasting me
and dancing on my grave... someday..."

And that is okay! More than okay... that is comforting...
I am part of the splendid miraculous weaving...
we are all the creators and the creation...
the weavers and the weaving...
while we are breathing and once we cease...
no separation... ever.

And so the magical weaving of sweet daddy-o continues
in this faraway emory village...
a village created by church and profession.
We thought again "he must be close" last week...
days of non-responsiveness, no food...
only quick moments of eye gazing...
no energy for anything but breathing
and whatever else he is up to in there.

But today he is back with smiles and interest
talking about needing to get out of "this setting"...
ready to "move these legs"...
"make my way further down."

It is so hard to know how to be with it all sometimes...
we've been re-thinking the whole medication trip.

A beloved of mine, who is also my 5 elements
acupuncturist, shone a light for me recently...
the poppie flower is the plant being used in this culture
to help people cross over...
and it has been used extensively in human history
for all sorts of remedies and assistance...

Right now in hospitals and hospice the poppies are
flowing! We call it morphine and it is a pink liquid...
the accepted and legal plant ally
working the "let go" nerve of journeyers far and wide!!!

We haven't really had an excuse to "administer" it
to daddy-o since he is in no pain...
only the occasional catheter change...
so his let go nerve is quite exposed compared to most.

And we really don't know what to do about it...
just start droppin' poppie magic whenever...?
No... that doesn't feel good.
We did try the "hiccup medication"
i think it is called thorazine... an anti-psychotic...
my brother reid calls it "a sledgehammer of a med"...
Hospice had been suggesting it for months and it did
knock out those mean ol hiccups... It also knocked sweet
daddy-o into the zombie "this must be it!" zone...
So will we give it to him again when he gets the hiccups...?
oh godgoddess it's so hard to know!!
Is he ready to let go...?

Because he has walked his path in a culture and time
that has given very little encouragement
to practicing the spiritual art of letting go...
not many opportunities allowed
to explore death while living...
avoiding the ultimate thing we cannot control
simply because it is out of our control...

"eek! - nothin' we can do about that,
might as well not look over there"...
and so the sweet poppie
darning the death parade of our times...
helping a culture founded in control
open to the ultimate uncontrollable...

do you want that daddy-o...?
are you ready to go...?
just can't quite release your grip...?
is it fear or love keeping you here...?
will we ever know...?
your mystery is yours...
your journey so precious to honor...
and as your mid-wives we have questions...

while holding those questions
i suppose we just have to resign ourselves
that the answers might have to be
wild guesses...
and come to think of it...
you're probably fine with that, aren't you daddy-o...
you always liked wild guesses anyway.

here's to the mystery and the ancestors and the weaving...
with gratitude for all!!
lovelovelove

41... DARINGLY MIRACULOUS OR MIRACULOUSLY DARING

Nov 8... the chilly mornings have arrived
asking for an extra layer...
it is an interesting contrast as i feel that spiritually
i have been releasing layers...
layers of unconscious protection... automatic reaction...
layers of expectations and assumptions...
so sure i know how it is...NOT!!

Living in peru for 5 years basically splayed me open...
a belief system autopsy...
me just kind of lying there... allowing it all...
knowing it's good for me even though extremely
uncomfortable at times... oooey gooey innards eeek!...
the recipe including a good enough dose
of joy and adventure to keep me keepin' on...
enough psychic and synchronistic signs
– what i call soul talk –
whispering that i was exactly
where i was supposed to be...

And all the while... because i was so immersed
in the incredible self-awareness journey...
i did not have the perspective to really see what was
happening... Gotta step out of the expanding swirl for a
minute to look in and understand from a more intellectual
level... creating a holistic realization... the Big Bang!
(the one miracle science allows... funny, eh?)
And it is a miracle!!

When i look at my funny quirky kooky broken split
jagged edged path i've been walkin' these 49 years...
i am overwhelmed by the miraculous!
And perhaps the biggest miracle of all is Now...
this timing... to follow the peruvian autopsy
by landing within my blood circle...
my parents my brothers their wives
my nephews and niece... my tap root community...
providing all the footnotes to the open book...
glimpses into the origins of now exposed nerves...
snapshots of the energetic patterns that fed me
and wrapped me in utero and beyond –
in both directions… all directions... whooosh!!
Awe!

Yesterday while carol the hospice nurse was
visiting i asked daddy-o if he wanted some
scrambled eggs and cheese toast...
he responded by saying something about
"she knows it all through relationship"...
then he said
"the circles are saying it is time for completion"...
he asked "what do you think of that?"...

carol responded that she thought it was the right thing...
daddy-o said "so we have one positive vote"...
then he asked "do you feel daring?"...
carol said yes and asked if he did...

eyebrows lifted eyes bulging strong voice of clarity
daddy-o said "Yes!"

To dare...
he nailed it as usual!!
To dare is really what it is all about!...

So many moments during this midwifing vigil when i have
had to muster all the dare up from my daring reserve...
and daddy-o knows it...
the daring to allow the cracking...
the daring to look at my dependencies
and contributions to unhealthy family patterns...
to re-evaluate anything and everything...
and the daring to trust...
trust that even though i don't know what i am doing...
somewhere in me i do know what i am doing...
the daring to trust that... all - is - well - all - the - time!!

And I am so grateful for my peru life...
for the daring i am pulling on now was fed in peru...
if i hadn't dared there I wouldn't be so daring now
when it is sooo important and potent!

According to Diane Dunn from her book,
Cusco: the gateway to inner wisdom,
in Andean cosmology
"To Dare" is a sacred word
and part of the chacana - the andean cross -
associated with the south and the element fire...
To Dare
is to step outside of our comfort zone
so we might grow and know ourselves more....

To Dare
is to allow fire to burn away our fears and worries and
insecurities... burning excuses or emotions that keep
us from embracing transformation... transformation into
more light-filled beings with spiritual fire so we might
dare to bring compassionate action into the world.

Did daddy-o nail it or what?!!!!

And of course he is being asked To Dare
waywayway! waywayway! waywayway! more than me...
and so now I, and all of us surrounding him,
have the opportunity to absorb some of that
daring energy...
just by being in his presence and watching
with open hearted acceptance... witnessing his
daring journey even when the struggle of it makes
one want to turn away or medicate it away...
keep looking... keeping being present... keep on keepin'...
the daring reserve is being filled!

And beyond our small circle daddy-o is streaming his
daring out into the world... as he always has...
the love dare... the christ dare...
I dare you to be christ...
I dare you to walk through this fear filled jagged edged
world with loving kindness and compassionate joy...
to illuminate the darkness with a fire of love...

Thank you daddy-o! Thank you christ! Thank
you peru! Thank you sweet mystery!
Daringly miraculous or miraculously daring... you all are!
lovelovelove

42... LOMO NEGRO

my sweet dog friend, lomo negro...
the most elegant savvy wise handsome fella
i have ever had the good fortune to know
as my shadow guardian admirer...

truly i have never felt such a burning focus
of adoration and esteem...
his eyes and heart potent windows
guiding me deeper into the mysteries of his village...

he truly is of inkan nobility...
an enlightened being whose sweet nibbles tickled my
spirit and patient gentle knowing held me tender...
a life-saver for this gringa!!

he died this morning...
he was wow's companion for 12 years...
the 5 years i lived with them he got good and spoiled
and he loved it...
i love you lomo... so sorry i wasn't there...
come visit me in my dreams... please.

Through meeting those on the other side,

we get a precious glimpse of the grandeur and beneficence

of the inner universe.

More important, contact stimulates inner life

and brings us into familiarity with our greater spiritual identities.

Our greater identities are living demonstrations

of a more inclusive kind of good,

the kind that flows from the well-spring of spontaneity and self-trust.

So when the dead talk back, listen.

-The Last Frontier;

Exploring the Afterlife and Transforming Our Fear of Death.

by Julia Assante

43... COMPOST

Sunday Nov 16th... sitting at the counter of my favorite
coffee house... mocha with almond milk buzz helping
me stretch to the surface of awakeness...
the day is cloudy as is my brain...
oh well such it is... i like cloudy days...
probably don't get too many cloudy days in heaven...
the world of energy... the other side...
whatever we want to call it.
I feel like we don't really have the appropriate language...
if heaven didn't have so much baggage
attached to it I would more easily use it.
There is always the idea that using the old words within our
new consciousness will somehow release the baggage... sort
of changing-the-system-from-within idea... and perhaps.

I for one love the idea of compost
- one of my greatest spiritual teachers -
the breaking down of the old creating vibrant nutrients
for the new to sprout and grow...
the decomposition of the physical material allowing
the energy to return to soil... or source.

The real challenges of this teacher called compost are...
#1- the realization of the expiration... really being able to
discern when something is no longer healthy and useful...
no longer serving its purpose...
and #2 - the acceptance of said realization leading to
action... letting go of the old food or the old belief system
or the old habit... and placing it into the compost bin...

or in daddy-o's case... the old body...
getting closer and closer to being ready for the bin.
"oh me"... such a thing to be witnessing!
especially with the intimacy of our view...
me and mama were cleaning him up this morning
and the question was "oh... perhaps the kidneys are
starting to break down...?" and with such a question...
in our minds... we tip the boulder that is barely balancing
and send it rolling down the hill.

It is what is supposed to be happening...
things are supposed to start breaking down...
but oh Shit! we are not used to such... our knee jerk
reaction is to fix it... fix it until the options of fixing become
absurd... until the dead end sign bangs us in the face...
or the boulder rolls us over.
And since we are not choosing that option... we then are
allowing and thus intimately watching the composting of
sweet daddy-o's body! FUCK!!... are we sure about this?!
the boulder is really rolling...
we cannot stop it... turn away?... no, we must watch it...
compassionate witnesses... staying as present
and conscious as we can... honoring his work as
he is as present and conscious as he possibly
can be to what is happening to his body...
himself a compassionate witness.

our sweet cousin david crossed over a week ago today...
he was 42 with a beloved wife and two young daughters...
he and his family, encouraged by the medical system,
pushed that boulder back as long as they could.
And of course! They had to.
sometimes it is how we have to do it...

and our current medical system caters to this need…

There is a time and place for everything… sometimes
we must push back and sometimes we must release,
let it roll… and always the challenge for loved ones
is the same… to be compassionate witnesses
as the boulder does what it is going to do.
and I can't imagine being tara, david's wife… her
challenge as a compassionate witness far greater than
what i am experiencing… his daughters!… "oh me"…
please send them your loving thoughts and prayers.

And even while it is so hard to watch…
i have no doubt in my heart that david is home now…
as is coleman… as is my sweet dog friend lomo negro…
daddy-o will be there soon too.
And that that home isn't some other place…
the composting of their material selves
completely allowing their energy to release…
no longer constricted by the density of body…
their energy returning back to source…
soil… god… the All…
which is right here right now…
the only separation a matter of perception.

Just before I got the word from peru that my dog friend
lomo had died… I was sitting with daddy-o and out
of the blue he said, "there's a dog on the screen."
He was looking down towards the end of his bed
and slightly over towards the dresser…
no dog on screen in the air there…
that I could perceive anyway…
lovelovelove

44... "BOUNDARIES, WINNDY, BOUNDARIES!"

wednesday dec 3... very cliche and it draws
the best picture describing the notion...
when the air pressure in the plane drops and
the oxygen masks fall you must place yours
on your face first and foremost... only after you
have full lungs can you then assist others...
or as my first counselor 20 years ago or so put it
- your cup must be full before you share...
once full the overflow can be constant and abundant...
flowing out to all you encounter... indeed.

unfortunately i have been feeling unable to fill my cup
the past few months and so not at all being of service
in an easy and joyful way...
more like "okay how much frickin' longer!?"
feeling resentful and anxious...
resentful at the unconscious patterns of relating and
reacting that i cannot yet keep from draining me...
all families have them i suppose...
these old connections
that get established between family members...
really at birth
and back then they were probably fine and appropriate...
but if not held in a light of conscious awareness
therefore allowed flexibility...
they can become cement veins blocking
healthy growth and expansion...
holding us in old stagnant connections.

for the past 20 years i have been doing constant
spiritual growth work
ie. bringing the unconscious that is within me
to a place of more consciousness...
shining light into my shadows...
vomiting up diseased beliefs of myself and others...
examining it all.
and none of those countless workshops or ceremonies
have come close to the intensity of sitting in the
old patterns like i have been doing here...
seeing the ball of ancestral yarns as they twine through
grandparents long gone from the physical plane yet
well represented via these energetic threads...
encircling mom and dad, my brothers, nephews and nieces
and of course me...

In the world of spiritual awareness the work can be
compared to peeling the layers of an onion...
one has no clue the depth of the layers and what might
be under the top until each layer is exposed bit by bit...
sometimes an arduous process... sometimes really easy...
and it's the work of a lifetime...
each new layer that gets exposed
shows how little i know...
how much unconsciousness still resides in me.

Well these past 9 months of living with my
beloved parents has exposed many layers...
and i am super grateful for the exposure and learning
- it's been immense!!!!
and i'm pooped!

if i could just accept the threads and not feel a need
to work to untangle and resist it might be fine...
but that is where the anxiousness comes in...
the threads do not feel healthy for me anymore...
i've gained 25 pounds
and feel 20 years older than when i arrived...
Eeek!

Now certainly some of that is the cultural threads of this
country... i didn't just return to my family's patterns
but also culture shock bang zing clobber daze...
and again - amazing insight because of it all...
and did i already say - i'm pooped!!!

So in an attempt to take care of myself
I have decided to shift my living situation.
I have spiritual family living in athens, ga
and they have invited me to come and live with them...
it feels too obvious to not acknowledge and act upon...
and at the same time it is really hard.
Gatra is worn out as well...
though i must say her stamina is incredible!!...
and so i feel sad to be leaving her and, of course,
super hard to tear myself away from sweet daddy-o.
I will commute into the big city to be with them 4 to 5 days
a week... so i will still be very present and involved
just not living in it.
And even though i haven't even made the move yet...
already things feel so much lighter and more balanced
and I already feel healthier!...
just by saying Yes! to the restorative opportunity...
giant gratitude to <u>Jean</u> and <u>Don</u> and their daughter Sophia
for opening their home and hearts!!!

Whereas for the past month or so daddy-o and i have had okay to semi-sour connections... since deciding to move a few days ago he and i have been singing and laughing and watching charlie chaplin... while reflecting on his life... as he was born into the era of charlie's movies... speaking to the wonderful time he has had and his gratitude for it all...

I haven't even told him that i am moving out yet... he can just feel the shift in my energy and that shifts everything else... we are both extreme empaths so if one of us is slightly off kilter... well, it's more. And with mama as well... just since our talk about it we are having a much better connection. She is being very supportive!...

daddy-o always has said to me "boundaries, winndy, boundaries!"... most certainly one of my bigger life lessons is having appropriate boundaries... and so here it is... i'm tryin' sweet daddy-o... learning from your example...

he always made sure his cup was full... it was his life discipline... his daily structure and morning routine... and because of it he was, and still is, able to abundantly flow out to all those he encounters... oh that someday i might come close to his level of this ability... yet another skill he accomplished along his marvelous path... another teaching from the bag of his masterful wisdoms... thanks daddy-o!... i'm trying... and dangit!... it's hardest of all putting up the boundaries with You! lovelovelove

Until the day the earth starts turnin' right to left

Until the earth just for the sun denies itself

Until dear mother nature says her work is through

Until the day that you are me and I am you.

- Stevie Wonder,"As"

45... MYSTICAL ADVENT IN DR.SUESS

Dec 15... Here we are in the season of Advent...
the waiting, the anticipating, the knowing
and therefore manifesting... the Coming!...
of what?... a historical figure swaddled up
and laying in a manger..??
perhaps...
especially if we want to take the easy route...
it's not about us... it's about him...
"oh good... i just have to go out and buy things to show my
giving spirit… hang out with the fam and eat lots of food"...
it's a start I suppose...
and what if really the point to propose is a wee bit more...
possibly a consciousness challenge
I can embrace and adore..?
Woe-HoHoHO! What say you sweet daddy-O..?
(beggun' your pardon —lots of dr.suess
in my auditory periphery)...

As so I am, living in a whole-heartedly different home these
days... Instead of no flame allowed... now it is consistent
tending of flame as a wood fire warms the cozy.
Instead of no critter friends allowed... now it is two
dogs, three cats and oodles of chickens needing
consistent assistance in portal opening, for their desire
to shift from the in to the out is quite frenetic…
(anyone have an old doggie door for sale or trade?)
Instead of witnessing the sundown process of
an elder... now it is dancing with a toddler in the
rays of her sunrise... dr. suess and all.

And remarkable in this home shift... most of all... is
the energy of my heart space as it embraces the here
and now. Sitting with daddy-o is Now a treat to look
forward to... visiting with mama and hearing the details
of the Here a more welcomed receiving... I set my
intention as i drive the mileage and so then step into the
waiting container with more clarity and discipline...
like an artist stepping into her studio...
but i am a mystic stepping into an advent vortex
of unlimited possibilities and energies...
Ooh wee!
sounds much better than "care-taking my dad"
doesn't it..!? And it is truly my truth.

A wonderful book called "The Last Frontier - Exploring
the After-life and Transforming Our Fear of Death" has
been accompanying me for months. The author, Julia
Assante, introduced me to the new quantum computer...
did y'all know there is such...?
"So when you submit something to it for calculation,
it will compute that calculation in 256 dimensions,
meaning 256 different universes,
on 256 different computers simultaneously.
Consequently what could take a conventional computer
many millions of billions of years to find out would
take a quantum computer about twenty minutes"...
Yeeeedawgie!
the ball game is a-changing!
The uni-verse is morphing into a multi-verse...
But wait!... it's not the universe that's changing...
it's our Perspective that is morphing...
our Consciousness that is expanding!...

Bring on the Advent!! It's coming!!
The New Human!
WE- as a collective - are the swaddled infant!
One can say, "Beggn' your pardon... did you say Homo
sapien? Oh-hoho... how passe... please please can't you
see... I'm Homo Luminous, indeed!"... the fabulous fusion
of science and spirit calling it out... otherwise known as...
drum roll please... the wildly anticipated...
often overlooked... wildly mistook... confused and confined
in institutions of divine... it's the one... the only...
Christ Consciousness, don't you know!!!!!...
give it up y'all!!!...the Super C.C. holy known...
Christ made manifest in the Whole!!...
Hole in One!
Baamm!
And thus advent becomes a wee bit more exciting...
don't you agree!?
And a wee bit more challenging...
it is about You as a part of the We...
not just about some cool note-worthy historic He.

Daddy-o has been enjoying the sense, the scents,
the sights of advent mostly via the christmas tree...
and perhaps using it to skip between dimensions...
touring the multi-verse as it might be.
and as I come in to sit with him... I open as wide
as wide can be.... to perhaps journey with him
or interpret his wanderings with a mystical wondering.
Yesterday he said to me,
"like those circles at the top of the christmas tree"...
staring and staring I so want to see... he describes for me
"a small circle inside a larger one... white and open,
can't you see?"

151

Ahhhh yes! the star or angel at the top of the pyramid...
the steeple reaching with yearning... inviting... opening the
portal... luminous halo streaming in... flagging the arrival...
Christ is Here!
All those years I never noticed...
thank you daddy-o!!... I see it now!...
the sweet triangle evergreen
rocking the "mas de christ"...
so bold yet humble as an adorned and illuminated pyramid
channeling in... bringing in from the multi-verse wide...
the spirit and light of love divine! woe-hoho!...
there is always so much more to the little slice of what we
see... 256 dimensions the quantum computer decrees!

And so this is me... I interpret what others might call
dementia or death-bed-confusion as possible windows...
sneak peeks into a broader perspective...
mystical lenses of potential illumination...

I called the other day while driving down the expressway
and mama immediately said let me call you back...
soon after, she did saying "well your father says
he is in the middle of the expressway"...
Oh but it is me!... i'm driving down the expressway...
he just transported somehow to here with me...
perhaps only psychically... only!?

Also, my friend Bloom Post, a shamanic healer, made
a kind offer to send some of her energetic being friends
to work with me... well I didn't notice much but sweet
daddy-o did!...and being the kind host of gentile degree…

he was insisting that mama feed his 6 guests bowls of
soup as they were seated around him in a jolly circle...
some might say imaginary friends...
but I think not.
And as daddy-o has delighted me with such spirit realm
wanderings... he also has been less likely to know it is me...
a few days ago as i entered his wreath and stood at
the foot of his bed... he said in reply to how ya doin?
"well just fine, waiting for your sister winn to arrive"...
i said "oh daddy-o, it's me, i'm winn"...
he said eyes wide and big big smile, "well glory be!"

And mama's having to introduce herself in the mornings
as his gaze informs her there's a lack of recognition...
but once fully awake he doesn't forget throughout the
day... calling her by name over and over just to have her
sit by his side or to announce his hearty appetite...
food is still, or even more than ever, a great delight!

He also remembers quite easily the lyrics to the carols
as we sing sing sing...
"sle-ep in hea-venly peace"...

So fascinating to watch his back and forth... his in and
out... his perspective shifts and expanding awareness...
transformation as ordinary and extraordinary...
something we are all doing... after all - advent tells us so.

So a grace-filled advent and holy-day season to you all,
beloved friends family community tribe...
whatever the coming event means for you...
may it fill your heart and spirit with wonder and delight!
lovelovelove

46... YOU AND I ARE ONE

A Solstice Kiss... going out to all my beloveds...
down yonder in the deep deep south it is
summer solstice...
the light bright fuels fire of growth and abundance...

while in my northern home the bare branches outlined
by an early sunset remind me of sleepy, craggy limbs
exposed without the cover of youthful decor...
standing strong and naked
as old man winter blows the bones.

Feeling the contrast...
the duality of human awareness here on planet earth...
marvel-us in joy and despair.

And then i send my attention up and out into the
starry wonder as a dark moon reminds me of love's
expansive power re-membering sweet Coleman...
and as I float with him the expansion rips my perspective
out beyond the confines of this wee petri-dish...
with its heavy belief systems and dense judgments gone...
I AM...
resting with him in one heart... the heart...
no contrast here...
he and i equally alive and equally dead...
for neither exists... all is all...
'a' met 'h' and they said deep sigh ahhhh!

Daddy-o was so excited to see me yesterday
and after joyful greetings he asked...
and who are you...??

His body slightly flinched when i said I'm winn...
and he asked, "how do i know you as winn...?"
after a few minutes pondering, i said...
well what does your heart tell you...
do you feel a familiar flicker in your heart...?
does it feel comfortable to be in my presence...?
he gazed deeply into my eyes for many moments...
i said, in your heart do you feel me...?
in your heart are we one...?
staring deep into each other via our crystal windows...
he repeated my questions as statements...
perhaps he felt it... i sure did!
Daddy-o and i are one and we have eternity...
Coleman and i are one and we have eternity...
You and i are one and we have eternity....

As so i dance ferociously in the stimulating confusion
of light and dark... eating voraciously from the plate of
good and bad... knowing myself wrapped in the chaotic
garb of feminine potential by allowing the masculine
spear of conscious intent to slay me open so that creator
might see creator's reflection within our outpouring
of conscious love design... duality into unity...
the two becoming one...
light and dark melting into neither...
life and death resting in the same beating heart...
on this solstice i remember... this is my reality...
the call of the mystics ringing constant...
and so it is… the bell i choose to answer.
and whatever bell might be tickling your fancy today...
may its vibration caress you in the vital energy
of love divine!!!
lovelovelove

I lift up my eyes to the hills.

From whence does my help come?

² My help comes from the Lord,

who made heaven and earth.

³ He will not let your foot be moved,

he who keeps you will not slumber.

⁴ Behold, he who keeps Israel

will neither slumber nor sleep.

⁵ The Lord is your keeper;

the Lord is your shade

on your right hand.

⁶ The sun shall not smite you by day,

nor the moon by night.

⁷ The Lord will keep you from all evil;

he will keep your life.

⁸ The Lord will keep

your going out and your coming in

from this time forth and for evermore.

-Psalm 121

47... AMEN

Well...
sweet daddy-o finally did it y'all!!

He let go... transitioned... is journeying home.
His last breath was at 7:05pm.

All was peaceful and beautiful.
Please send him prayers of love and celebration...
ease and acceptance.
We will keep him here at home for the night...
sit with him... absorb him... sing to him...
tend to him... breathe for him...

Behold... a Christmas light is shining brightly... Amen.

December 23, 2014

48... DADDY-O'S CHRISTMAS GIFTS OF AMAZEMENT

Dec 27... and the prayer continues a wee bit longer...

firstly... to inform as folk are asking... our beloved bill mallard's material temple will be returned to sweet mother earth next saturday, jan 3... we will meet at turner funeral home at 10 am and process to westview cemetery for a graveside service at 11am... then later that same day we will gather at glenn united methodist church for a memorial celebration service at 2pm with a reception following... all who might feel compelled to join us are, of course, warmly welcomed.

secondly... to share the amazing christmas gifts that sweet daddy-o delivered on his way up and out...

the last several weeks he had been talking about wanting to go home pretty consistently...
last saturday his grandson edison was playing on the bed next to him and daddy-o said "i'm needing to get on home"... edison said, "you are home"... daddy-o stared blankly and then i said "maybe he means another home... daddy-o do you mean another home?"... he turned to me and held my gaze... i heard a big Yes! in his eyes...

He also was losing his language... his speech... which was probably his favorite of all things human... And he could tell it was slipping... the words not coming with the eloquent ease he'd always known... and in some of those blank moments we could feel his shyness or dismay thus sadness filled the room where normally it had stayed a bay...

159

Also the christmas season played such a perfect lullaby...
gorgeous carols in twinkling tree lights
rocking him into release.

He loved christmas... he loved jesus...
he loved singing... and well the three combined!...
that was his supa-deluxe hot fudge sundae style treat!...
especially when a good crowd was joining in.
And this deluxe sundae was delivered to him every
christmas eve service as he led the opening carols
- featuring his signature song "the amen
chorus" –introducing the pageant performance
at his beloved glenn memorial...
The church folk had been in a stir as to what could
happen this year instead and decided to ask my brothers,
reid and rob, to stand in for daddy-o. A few weeks
prior reid and rob told sweet daddy-o of the honor they
had received and his response was very telling... he
was deeply distressed... like it had just hit him... the
realization brought up before him in vivid technicolor...
he wasn't gonna get his super yummy christmas treat
this year... and thus the joyful carols turned lullaby...
falala's blanketed in muffled melancholy.

The night before his transition he had a fever
which lasted into the morning and was then joined by the ol'
burdensome hiccups... mama was concerned but decided
a blocked catheter (we'd had many) was the culprit and
the hospice nurse was called to come and solve the issue.
Daddy-o was sort of groaning after each hiccup but every
time mama asked if he was in pain or uncomfortable he
said No, which turned out to be his only word that day.

Mid-day his fever broke and by late afternoon the hiccups vanished and he seemed to be sleeping peacefully... probably thanks to the mighty thorazine that was brought in for relief... (and very likely 'the release'). early evening about 6:15 mama was in the kitchen... heard a sort of shout/groan from the bedroom and went rushing in... about the same time carol the hospice nurse arrived... daddy-o's breathing was strained and full of effort... rob describes it as a panting... mama calls it chain-stoke breathing... She sent out the call to us all...

I was in Athens at the copy shop making my last minute gifts... she said we're definitely close... carol says 24 - 48 hours... I gathered up my copies, headed home, walked in the door... mama called again this time saying he just stopped breathing but his heart is still beating... i'll hold the phone up to his ear so you can talk to him...

and so i did...

dropping deeply into my heart
and with all the sweet love i could muster
i whispered...
"oh sweet daddy-o... you did it!
you're going home!
all is well!
i love you so much!
i'll see you again soon."
over and over and over and over and over and over again...
for eternity.

then i drove through the rain...

when I arrived i heard more of the story...

mama and alison (reid's wife) were on one side
and on the other rob sat singing...
"rob sang him across" mama said...
he started with "precious lord lead me home"... went
through a few others and it was during his signature
"amen chorus" that sweet daddy-o took his last breath...

and apparently that last expiration was a doozy...
he squinched up his face like he was straining...
mustering up all of his spiritual gel...
and then with relief release allowance...
he let out a long long sigh... it was a note... a tone...
he sang his last breath
and it went on for 30 to 40 seconds...

then a pulse for a few more minutes...
then peace.

mama said over and over... "what a gift! what a gift!
he went so easily once it was time... what a gift!"

we had already decided we would keep him with us for
a bit and tend him ourselves... so after a few hours reid
and mama and i washed his body... rubbed him in oil...
brushed his teeth (for he loved it so)... combed his hair...
gave him a shave...
thanking his sweet body temple for carrying
his mighty soul so well and so long...
dressed him and wrapped him in the white blanket that had
been his faithful servant since he had taken to his bed.

then I sat up with him all night... meditating... praying...
envisioning his flight.

the next day church folk came to visit...
everyone is saying sweet daddy-o wasn't about
to miss his beloved christmas eve service
and door number 1 was the only choice...
so he took it.

reid and rob wrestled with whether or not to go ahead and
participate in daddy-o's stead and thankfully decided so...
and thus the conduit was put in place...
the channel obvious and open...
and by goodness! daddy-o showed up y'all!!...
like, he was In da Hooowse!...

reid and rob's earnest, heartfelt and wonderful conducting
of a number of favorite carols created the perfect cauldron
so daddy-o's spark might ignite...
his oh so special spark of divine enthusiasm
- his precious gift.

then rob surprised us all by asking me to get up
and join the finale "amen chorus"...
already a super ecstatic spiritual tellin' the story...
"see the little baby... amen... layin' in a manger... amen...
on christmas morning... amen amen amen!"...
and with a young member from the church,
Geoffrey Solomon, sounding out the verses just right
in daddy-o's stead...
everyone clapping and singing our little hearts out...
filling the grand sanctuary with anguished adoration...
we sang it out!...

amen!
the sacred word of old.
amen!... a cry for closure...
amen!... a cry for continuation...
amen!... filling ourselves with god...
amen!... filling ourselves with daddy-o...
AMEN!!!

Overwhelmed! my tender heart was cracking wide open...
feeling daddy-o so strong...
feeling his love for his church family...
feeling his love for his most cherished guide,
his beloved, jesus...
feeling his love of bringing joyful song to the people...
feeling his love of love...
feeling my tears of love.

At the last Amen!
the packed house jumped to their feet
Standing Ovation!!!!!
goosebumps flooded my skin
as the telltale cheers of enthusiasm rose up
filling the sanctuary...
lifting the roof!...
it was all i could do not to shatter into a million pieces
grief joy ecstasy sorrow wonder... amazement!!!!...
Daddy-o is Here!!!!!

It is all so truly amazing!...
death is a miracle...
resurrection so very real.

thank you daddy-o!
for these amazing christmas gifts...
and for all the many gifts you've shared with me
and so many others...

my heart will sing for you always.
lovelovelove

"Precious darling,

St. Therese was so captivated by the rose I gave you that she

has decided to preserve it forever and ever....with her...

in the special place of her spirit (see the picture!)

And so the same with our love, which is always and always.

I am so grateful for us. Thinking of you on this peaceful evening.

It is so serene here!

I love you, Bill"

-The gift to Gatra (in the form of this card) that appeared "out of nowhere"
on the floor of their bedroom a few days after Bill's transition.

St. Therese of Lisieux
(1873-1897)

Until recent times it was difficult to find a Catholic church without a statue of St. Therese of Lisieux. While statues seem less in vogue since Vatican II, this saint remains one of the most popular in the Roman Church. On one level she accomplished next-to-nothing in her brief life. When she died of tuberculosis at the age of 24, the prioress of her monastery wondered what she could possibly write in the obituary that would be sent to the other Carmelite monasteries. On a deeper level, Therese helped revolutionize modern Christian concepts of holiness.

She came from a bourgeois family and was a spoiled child. When two of her older sisters entered the local Carmelite monastery, she made up her mind to follow them. She received special permission to enter monastic life when she was only 15. Her remaining nine years were spent washing laundry, sweeping corridors and struggling to stay awake during meditation. After developing tuberculosis, she was appointed mistress of novices. The superior of the monastery also ordered her to write an account of her life, which has become one of the most widely read books on spirituality in modern times.

Therese described her vocation as simply LOVING – loving God and the world. Whereas many Christians had often suspected that being holy meant only something dramatic in the past – being eaten by lions, sitting for fifty years on top of a pillar, whipping oneself daily – Therese believed that doing one's ordinary work was quite enough, provided all was done with love. She strove in every way to identify herself with the people of her time. On a deeper plane this sharing was manifested in spiritual suffering, when she lost all sense of God's presence in her life during her last few years. She continued to embrace everything with generous love, including her fatal illness, in spite of the spiritual aridity that she felt. This darkness and aridity finally lifted in her last few minutes, and she died in ecstasy. She is depicted with roses as a symbol of the prayers she promised after her death.

Printed on recycled paper in Canada

GTL

Bridge Building Images, Inc.
P.O. Box 1048
Burlington, VT 05402
www.BridgeBuilding.com
© Robert Lentz

STE. THERESE DE LISIEUX

St. Therese of Lisieux

Icon painting by Brother Robert Lentz, O.F.M.

www.robertlentz.com

49... HERE LIES A GENTLE POWER

January 8th... Elvis' birthday... and I have been riding
with this passage from one of my new favorite books
- *The Wisdom Jesus* by Cynthia Bourgeault...
I can't say it any better right now...

"Blessed are those who mourn, for they will be comforted."

*Essentially, from a wisdom perspective, this second beatitude
is talking about vulnerability and flow. When we mourn we
are in a state of freefall, our heart reaching out for what
we have seemingly lost but cannot help loving anyway. To
mourn is by definition to live between the realms. "Practice
the wound of love," writes Ken Wilber in Grace and Grit,
his gripping personal story of loss and transformation.
"Real love hurts; real love makes you totally vulnerable
and open; real love will take you far beyond yourself; and
therefore real love will devastate you." Mourning is indeed
a brutal form of emptiness. But in this emptiness, if we can
remain open, we discover that a mysterious "something"
does indeed reach back to comfort us; the tendrils of our
grief trailing out into the unknown become intertwined
in a greater love that holds all things together. To mourn
is to touch directly the substance of divine compassion.
And just as ice must melt before it can flow, we, too,
must become liquid before we can flow into larger mind.
Tears have been a classical spiritual way of doing this.*

Oh my...thank you cynthia!

And so I am melting in the mourning... in the morning...
the crack of daybreak...
the slit between chapters...
the pause between inhalation and exhalation...

It's a wavy pause that melts me...
up down in out rolling between mind and heart...
JOY!!!... for daddy-o is home
and how wonderful it must feel for him!!...

TEARS!... as I feel his tenderness touching my tenderness...
the tenderness of all human-beings... as we wobble-
fwobble-hobble-along sharing the crack of vulnerability
while at the same time struggling to hide it from
each other... "oh pity!" cries the release...

this past weekend we had a friday night wake...
a saturday morning graveside...
then a saturday afternoon memorial celebration service...
it was a lot but at the same time not...
and it all went beautifully...
all of mama's careful orchestration paid off...
and all of daddy-o's careful and deliberate choices
he made as to how to live a loving life
found graceful expression upon exquisite altars...
altars witnessing with gratitude and humility
as well as humor and creativity...
it was a giant affair and at the same time oh so gentle...

Ordering his gravestone we were perplexed as to
what to say as space was very limited... rob in his
brilliance knew... "Here lies a gentle power"
lovelovelove

50... WHITE CRYSTAL HOLY ROUND

"oh me"... 2/12/2015... who would've seen it coming...
any of it!!
where i am... where daddy-o is... where coleman is...
where we all are... where humankind is!
we sort of see it all coming but really we don't.
During sweet daddy-o's long death march a few folk said
to me... "no matter how long a time you have to prepare,
it is still a shock when it happens."
They were so correct!

and i feel it is the same as i sit atop the sacred
appalachians peeping out at the world our
dominant consumer culture has created...
i know it is in its death march...
i've been midwifing its death for most of my life...
and still yet... once the transition happens i will be in
shock. I wonder why? Is it the "miracle effect"...?
Transitions that are divinely orchestrated...
outside the direct intervention of our small mind
ego selves...
no matter how prepared we are...
the shift waves shake us beyond anything we can
imagine... that is, if we are present, alert and aware...
The Miracle Effect.

i went hiking up the mountain the other day...
the night had brought frost and the sun had not yet
reached to thaw the upper realm of the northern slope...
as i was approaching the first thicket of frosted jewels
i was stopped in my tracks...

the sun was shining from behind the thicket...
its illumination was coupled with its warmth creating
one of the most stunning portraits i've ever seen...
Every tiny piece of tree of plant of leaf of shrub
was frosted and melting and shining
in the glow of its demise...

It was as if the entire forest was dotted with iridescent pin
points of light... mostly white light... occasional electric
blues... and less frequent blue with a green rim...
It took my breath away...
a daylight display of the best christmas
light scene imaginable...
I opened my eyes as wide as i could
standing as still as possible
drinking in the amazing sight presented before me...
glorious symphonic sculpture of fire and ice...

i wanted to capture it...
to will it into my memory... my heart... my being...
the accompanying soundtrack
dripdrop dripdrop... plop.

but, of course, i couldn't capture it or save it...
its beauty rested in its unsave-ableness...
in the process of melting...
that is where the stunning beauty made manifest...
in the process of each little frost flake dying to warmth...
in each pin point an astounding miracle is released...
is allowed... is born...
the re-birth of death told in infinite nature stories...

the little story of the little frost flake that emerged
from the stars and then with morning light, glided
away on the sun's rays... so simple... so profound.

as i continued climbing up into the frosted forest
the lights danced in different ways...
from one angle with my back to the sun there
were no lights... "is there no frost there?"
walking up and looking closely at the wee leaves and
twigs... "yes, these limbs are just as frosted and the
melting is happening but the illumination is not...
so i can't see...
the miracle hidden from me."...
no spotlight to turn the ordinary into extraordinary...
my perspective keeping me from seeing... indeed...
perspective and sight...
so entwined.

And so it is with sweet daddy-o... coleman too.
My perspective - a product of my belief system –
is the shroud covering them now...
I know they are not far...
and I know they are sending me messages...
yet i am standing with the sun to my back and so
cannot see them... my perspective is askew...
How frustrating for them, eh?
How frustrating for all of our beloveds who have transitioned...

I turned back facing the sun again and the magnificent
sparkles returned... a few new spectrums... a flash of red...
orange... dotted here and there within the explosion of
white crystals holy round...

then i turned back away from the illumination...
dull wet winter forest...

easier to behold in some ways...
not as heartbreaking in astounding amazement...
but "no! i want the heartbreak... i want the moment
of amazement even though it is fleeting...
i want the illuminated perspective
that opens my spirit to the miraculous!...
i want to witness to the miracle of melting...
to the miracle of death and re-birth...
to the glory of resurrection!"

And so there's my homework...
(how 'bout y'all...? *winkwink*)…
using my imagination
to envision myself
in a different web of perspective...
a different web of belief... expectation... and awareness…
this shift then countering the shock of the miracle effect...
si o no..?

and as i envision my old energetic web...
shifting and transforming...
dying and transitioning...
I birth a new perspective…
I breathe a new consciousness!

sending it out to you all...
to all humankind...
wrapped in oodles and oodles of gratitude and joy!
lovelovelove

Come into being as you pass away.

-Gospel of Thomas, logion 42; Translation by William R. Schoedel

¹⁷ Therefore, if any one is in Christ, he is a new creation;

the old has passed away, behold, the new has come.

¹⁸ All this is from God,

who through Christ reconciled us to himself

and gave us the ministry of reconciliation;

¹⁹ that is, in Christ God was reconciling the world to himself,

not counting their trespasses against them,

and entrusting to us the message of reconciliation.

-2 Corinthians 5:17-19 (RSV)

A Prayer…

Oh dear sweet daddy-o

I miss holding your hand…

here…

And I release you to go and be free

with eternity…

Please know that I am always open to your guidance and assistance

as I commit 100% to the fulfillment

of my highest divine purpose and mission…

Also know that your earthly footsteps lead me

Enthusiastically

on a path

Where the ultimate service to christ…

to unity…

Is putting my tender vulnerable heart

out into the world…

With authenticity and responsibility.

Thank you.

Goodbye for now soul friend, star brother,

Wonder being of mighty light.

See you on the other side.

Love always.

Amen.

CPSIA information can be obtained
at www.ICGtesting.com
Printed in the USA
LVOW12s0551230416

484980LV00001B/1/P